# Informers

## Policing, policy, practice

*Edited by*
Roger Billingsley, Teresa Nemitz
and Philip Bean

**WILLAN**
PUBLISHING

Published by:

Willan Publishing
Culmcott House
Mill Street, Uffculme
Cullompton, Devon
EX15 3AT, UK
Tel: +44(0)1884 840337
Fax: +44(0)1884 840251
e-mail: info@willanpublishing.co.uk

Published simultaneously in the USA and Canada by:

Willan Publishing
c/o ISBS, 5824 N.E. Hassalo St,
Portland, Oregon 97213-3644, USA
Tel: +001(0)503 287 3093
Fax: +001(0)503 280 8832

First published 2001

ISBN 1-903240-07-7

British Library Cataloguing-in-Publication Data
A catalogue record for this book is available from the British Library

Typesetting and page layout by Willan Publishing. Text set in Palatino.
Printed and bound by T.J. International Ltd, Padstow, Cornwall

# Contents

# List of figures and tables

## Figures

## Tables

# Foreword

## Sir John Evans

Information and intelligence have always been, and will remain, the most essential components of policing and, indeed, all law enforcement work. They are the lifeblood of every enquiry from the simplest of offences to the most complex organised crime or matter of national security.

Sources of information are many and varied, ranging from the everyday interaction of officers with the public, anonymous reports via the Crimestoppers scheme, the use of paid and unpaid informants from the criminal fraternity, to the Security Services' use of agents.

For a number of good reasons, a growing reliance has been placed on the police use of informers which is reflected in, for example, the Audit Commission's 'Helping with enquiries – tackling crime effectively' (1993). Intelligence-led policing is now the norm, with the use of informants a valuable source of the information required for the process.

The integrity of the use of informants has, however, led to questions from some about the validity of such methods. Concern has been fuelled by a perception of too much secrecy, coupled equally with high profile cases of corruption centering around the misuse of informants, at a time when the need for policing with integrity has never been more important.

Clearly, ensuring the adequate protection of information and managing issues of confidentiality, need to be balanced with the requirements of openness and appropriateness. The Crime and Disorder Act has brought with it an added impetus to this need and the requirements to share information with community safety partners will be hampered unless an atmosphere of openness, trust and proportionality prevails.

The issue of informers is vitally important and complex. This book seeks to draw together those complexities and provide an invaluable resource for both practitioners and academics alike. I hope the book will encourage debate and contribute towards the desire of the Police Service to ensure the ethical use of information supports its purpose to uphold the law fairly and with integrity.

Sir John Evans, OStJ, QPM, DL, LL.B
Chief Constable, Devon and Cornwall Constabulary
President, Association of Chief Police Officers
    of England, Wales and Northern Ireland

# Preface

## David A Wakenshaw

As chairman of the ACPO (Association of Chief Police Officers) National Informant Working Group I am delighted to be associated with this publication which will inform, enhance and develop the understanding of this critical area of law enforcement. The contributors are all experts within their own field and from their differing perspectives ensure that the topics are covered in great depth and with wisdom.

The book will be of interest to professionals both within and without the law enforcement area and will have particular relevance to practitioners in developing working practices. It is absolutely essential for the future of law enforcement that the ethical, professional and effective use of human intelligence sources is enhanced and encouraged. It is therefore incumbent on all practitioners to deal with this topic with total integrity and this publication should greatly assist this.

The future holds many challenges for law enforcement with the European Human Rights legislation on the immediate horizon and many technological advances testing our abilities to the full. These challenges must be met in a positive way and in the arena of informants many of these challenges will be extremely testing. It will be a measure of law enforcement how we meet these. I feel sure that they will be met and results achieved which will benefit the community we serve.

I wish this publication well.

David A. Wakenshaw
Assistant Chief Constable, National Crime Squad
Chair, ACPO National Informant Working Group

# Editors' preface

The editors would like to thank all the contributors for their assistance and for their obvious enthusiasm about this book which breaks new ground in British criminology. We hope it will be of use to practitioners and to all working or researching in the field. We would also like to thank those who gave us assistance, themselves informers or handlers, and all others who cannot be identified, yet who unstintingly gave their valuable time. For an under-researched area, often appearing forbidding to the outsider, it was gratifying that so many people were prepared to talk, and discuss what were often closely guarded secrets.

To these and colleagues in the Midlands Centre for Criminology and elsewhere we gratefully acknowledge their help and assistance.

Roger Billingsley, Teresa Nemitz, Philip Bean
September 2000

# Notes on the contributors

**Peter Bagshaw** is an Assistant Chief Constable with the North Yorkshire Police. He joined the police in 1979 as a graduate entrant and served in a cross-section of departments, both uniform and plain clothes. Whilst serving in the Nottinghamshire Police, he presented 'Crime Watch Midlands' on BBC2 television. He gained a Diploma in Applied Criminology from Cambridge University in April 2000.

**Carole Ballardie** is a Lecturer in social policy and social work at the University of Sussex. She worked as a main grade Probation Officer in London and East Sussex for 16 years, latterly as a joint appointment with Sussex University. Her research interests include youth justice studies, women in the criminal justice system, violent young women and girls.

**Philip Bean** is Professor of Criminology and Director of the Midlands Centre for Criminology and Criminal Justice at Loughborough University. He is the author or editor of eighteen books and many articles, mainly in the field of drugs and crime and mental disorder and crime. These include *Compulsory Admissions to Mental Hospitals* (John Wiley, 1980); *Mental Disorder and Legal Control* (Cambridge University Press, 1987) (with Pat Mounser); *Discharged from Mental Hospitals* (Macmillan, 1994); and forthcoming *Mental Disorder and Community Safety*. He has held Visiting Professorships in Canada, the USA and Australia. From 1995 to 1999 he was President of the British Society of Criminology.

**Alan Beckley** is the head of management development training in West Mercia Constabulary. He has written on the personal liability of police officers following major and critical incidents and is the editor-in-chief of *Police Research and Management*, a quarterly management journal for police officers.

**Roger Billingsley** is a recently retired police superintendent with 35 years' experience, mainly in criminal investigation. He has been an active member of the National Informant Working Group, and chairman of a research sub-group looking specifically at participating informers. Throughout his service he has been involved operationally with the use and management of informers, and has recently completed his Ph.D at Loughborough University on the relationship between informers and their handlers.

**Roy Clark** is a Deputy Assistant Commissioner for the Metropolitan Police Service, based at New Scotland Yard. He has completed 34 years' service, the major parts of which have been with the CID, and engaged in operations and investigations focused upon serious and organised crime. One of his present responsibilities is to oversee corruption enquiries and to devise and implement an anti-corruption strategy. He is a member of the ACPO Presidential Task Force on Corruption and chairs a working group of senior detectives from throughout the UK, thereby influencing the ACPO strategy on corruption. He has handled and controlled informers throughout his police career.

**Steven Greer** is a Reader in Law at the University of Bristol. He studied law at the University of Oxford and Queen's University Belfast, and sociology at the London School of Economics. He held appointments at Queen's University Belfast and at the University of Sussex before being appointed to a lectureship in law at Bristol. He is the author of two books, *Supergrasses: a study in anti-terrorist law enforcement in Northern Ireland* (1995) and *Abolishing the Diplock Courts: the case for restoring jury trial to scheduled offences in Northern Ireland* (1986, with A. White), together with a number of monographs, articles and contributions to collections of essays on issues in criminal justice and human rights.

**Bill Griffiths** is a Deputy Assistant Commissioner in the Metropolitan Police Service. He has recently been appointed Director of Serious Crime Operations with responsibility for all murder investigations and serious crime taskings. As a DCI he researched Crimestoppers in the US and was project manager for its implementation in London in 1988. He is now a member of the London Crimestoppers Board and chairs the ACPO working group on Crimestoppers, reporting to the intelligence sub-committee.

**Paul Iganski** is a Lecturer in Sociology and Criminology at the University of Essex. He is also a Visiting Scholar in the Brudnick Center for the Study of Violence and Conflict, Northeastern University, Boston, USA. He has carried out research in Britain and the United States and published articles on hate crimes and racist violence. His recent research focuses on moral dilemmas in punishing 'hate'.

**Alan Murphy** is a Detective Sergeant, and has been the co-ordinator of the London Crimestoppers Unit for 5 years. He is secretary to the ACPO working group and led the negotiations with the Crown Prosecution service on disclosure, his protocol on the subject being accepted by the crime committee without reservation.

**Teresa Nemitz** studied social policy and social administration at Nottingham University, and criminology and criminal justice at Loughborough University where she was awarded an M.A. and a Ph.D., the latter for a study on the use of appropriate adults by the police. She is a researcher, part-time lecturer and tutor at the Midlands Centre for Criminology and Criminal Justice, Loughborough University where her teaching includes courses on women and crime and policing. Her research interests are mainly in mental disorder, and crime, and drugs and crime, where she has published numerous papers.

**Peter Neyroud** is the Deputy Chief Constable of West Mercia Constabulary. He is the secretary of the National Committee on the Police Use of Firearms, Vice Chairman of the ACPO Committee on Human Rights and is leading the work on ethics in policing. He is a Fellow of the Royal Society of Arts, a member of IPPR's 'Forum on Criminal Justice' and a council member of Justice, the human rights organisation.

**Nigel South** is Professor of Sociology at the University of Essex. He has published seventeen books including the pioneering studies *Policing for Profit* (Sage, 1988) and (with N. Dorn and K. Murji) *Traffickers: drug markets and law enforcement* (Routledge, 1992). The latter was one of the first British studies to examine the importance of informers in drug law enforcement. Other books include *Drugs: cultures, controls and everyday life* (Sage, 1999); with R. Weiss (eds.), *Comparing Prison Systems* (Gordon and Breach, 1998); and with V. Ruggiero and I. Taylor (eds.), *The New European Criminology* (Routledge, 1998). He teaches in the areas of criminology and social policy and is also Director of the Health and Social Services Institute at the University of Essex.

**Tom Williamson** is the Deputy Chief Constable of Nottinghamshire Police. He joined the Metropolitan Police in 1966 and served in central and east London as a Detective Constable and Sergeant. He has served as Commandant of Hendon Police College, and as Chief Superintendent for East London with a particular interest in organised crime and murder investigations. His last post with the Metropolitan Police was as Commander responsible for crime matters in S.W. London. He took up the post of Assistant Chief Constable (Designated Deputy) in Nottinghamshire in 1995 and became the Deputy Chief Constable in 1999.

He gained a BSc (Hons) in psychology at the University of York in 1982 and a Ph.D in applied social psychology in 1989 at the University of Kent. He is visiting Professor at the Institute of Criminal Justice Studies, University of Portsmouth.

# Introduction

About one-third of all crimes cleared up by the police involve the use of informers; we think this alone justifies interest in a method of policing traditionally kept well out of public view. Policing, all sorts that is, would be impossible without informers; whether in its more traditional forms, or others such as in the military, or the Customs and Excise, or the State Security Services. All rely on informers to provide information about the world which they seek to control.

This book is mainly about a special type of informer, the professional informer, who gives information to the police in return for rewards – whether for money, for a lighter sentence, or for some other benefit. It is only occasionally about the so-called 'public-spirited' informers who give information because they see it as their duty to do so, and who seek no reward. In practice, however, the difference between them is less clear, and there is much overlap, for the professional can also be public-spirited and *vice versa*.

This book is also about those informers who are offenders, and who provide the police with information about others. It is about that murky world of half-truth, deception, innuendo and betrayal. The informer's identity is flawed, for as every school child knows, no one likes the 'telltale' or the 'snitch', but in the world of policing the informer provides valuable information about matters which the police could not otherwise obtain. That means the informer's identity must be honoured and protected, and the informer led to believe the relationship with the police officer is special, important, and based on trust.

Traditionally, the police have been reluctant to discuss the informer system, leaving it an unresearched area. Their reluctance is understandable, not least because protecting the informer's identity must be the foremost consideration. There is also the risk of having the police officer's own methods exposed and subjected to public scrutiny, and the accompanying risk of being shown to have been compromised by the informer, or being seen to behave in a way which invites criticism. Handling informers is a tricky business, often with a paper-thin line between the handler acting in an acceptable or non-acceptable manner. The best informers are those actively involved in crime, the so-called participating informers; but how much crime should they be allowed to commit? Or how much should the handler tell others about the informer's criminality? And should the handler take action on all types of information given to them, whether it be drugs, burglary or armed robbery? Traditionally, police deal with one type of crime and rarely use information given on others, yet withholding information is no less blameworthy than giving information that is false. The need for clear guidelines is obvious, but these are rarely enough. Training and integrity in handlers are also necessary.

For the professional informer the financial rewards are often paltry, unless that is a large reward is offered after a high-profile property offence, or a terrorist attack; even then payments can usually only be made after a successful conviction, and that could be weeks or months away. Most police forces have a central fund which is awarded by the police authority: a medium-sized police force would have a fund of about £50,000; that is for the whole of the force, and for all crimes, which must last a year. A typical payment is about £50.

Who then are these informers? Answering this apparently simple question is more difficult than it may seem and casts us into that world of truth and half-truth. For example, in a study of drug dealing in Nottingham one of us (PB) noticed how some dealers claimed to be informers when they were not, or claimed not to be when they were. And some claimed to be giving false information but said they were accepted by the police as informers. All the drug dealers claimed they knew the informers – but that may not be true either, and all wanted it known that any information they gave was in the public interest, not their own. Determining the truth in these circumstances is an uphill task.

Nor is the world of the so-called public-spirited informer any easier to unravel. Whilst many provide important information others are less welcome. Dorn, Murji and South (1992) talk of a small number of public-spirited informers called 'police buffs' who see themselves as amateur policemen and whose information is greeted by the police with 'weary dismay' (*ibid*: 123). Their information is rarely of value, and within this group malice and self-aggrandisement are as common as with the professional informer. Nor are all public-spirited informers prepared to co-operate fully; rarely do they want to testify in court, allow the police to mount surveillance operations from their property, or offer help that would implicate or involve them further. The obvious fear of reprisals, and of having time taken up by apparently needless court appearances are the often-stated reason for this reluctance. Nonetheless, assessing the motives of all informers, public-spirited or professional, is a *sine qua non* for all police officers: information may be part of a larger plan designed to trap the unwary police officer in some way.

In essence the fundamental differences between the public-spirited informer and the professional may have less to do with motives, more to do with the special relationship the informer has with the handler. A level of functional dependency develops which is important to both sides. For the police the informer provides information which would not be available otherwise, for the informer the relationship can produce a more lenient sentence, or perhaps an additional income, or satisfy the various psychological demands the informer may have, including his relationship with the police. It is the strength of this relationship that can determine the quality of the information provided.

The informer is a witness, albeit a special type of witness, but a witness nonetheless. Even this can be slightly misleading, however, as some informers may not give evidence in court, and in the strict legal sense are not witnesses, though like other witnesses they provide information. Encouragement is always given to witnesses to come forward, and to provide information, but it seems more and more of us are reluctant to do so. Television programmes emphasise the importance of giving information and seem to be relatively successful in relation to certain types of crime, but they do so by packaging and wrapping it as entertainment.

When children provide that information the matter becomes additionally complicated. The basic question is: should the police encourage children to act as informers? If so, should those children be registered informers, i.e. be paid and placed on a local police register with all that involves? And does it make a difference if the information provided is about members of their family? Most of all, should payments be made if the child is, say, a known substance-abuser or has an addiction to gambling? Some police officers believe that children should not act as informers, and not be registered; others say it depends on the information provided, and on who the offender is. A classic case history would be of 'a child aged 14 who informs against his father and his father's associates who are persistent burglars. The child is paid for the information and uses the money to play the slot machines'. There may be something ethically wrong and morally distasteful about encouraging a child to inform on his family, but that has to be set against the reduction of crime, especially of serious offences. Essentially the debate centres on whether children should be used for some greater end or whether they should be exempt because they are children? There are no easy answers to these questions, but we think they need to be raised and not quietly swept aside, or ignored.

Children are not of course the sole providers of information against the family: wives inform on husbands (we have never heard of a case where husbands inform on wives) and brothers on brothers. Relatives inform on relatives, and friends inform on friends, as do business associates on business associates. The informer system illustrates the full extent of human betrayal, whether it is a case of a one-off piece of information being passed on through spite where a neighbour informs on someone who is claiming benefit but working at the same time; or a young adolescent informing on someone who relieved her of her boyfriend; or the lengthy and persistent informer who informs on other offenders. The latter, usually an offender himself, punctures the so-called dictum that there is 'honour among thieves'. Another dictum similarly in need of questioning is the common notion that women inform because they are deceitful and spiteful. This rarely stands up to scrutiny. 'A bloke will do the same thing and for the same reason' (quoted in Dorn, Murji and South: 131).

In this Introduction we would like to outline some of the major features surrounding the use of informers as they relate to the main themes of this book. Firstly we provide a brief overview of some of the main legal issues involved followed by an examination of the way informers are handled. This section then closes with an overview of the Human Rights Act (1998) as it affects the use of informers. Secondly, we provide an outline and summary of the key themes of the contributions included in the book, and then end with a short commentary on the directions in which we think future research on informers could take.

## Legal issues

There is no legislation governing the use of informers but there are legal precedents and Home Office Guidelines. The use of informers was given the approval of none other than the Lord Chief Justice:

> For many years it has been well recognised that the detection of crime was assisted by the use of information given to the police by members of the public. Those members might be either professional informers who gave information regularly in the expectation of financial or other reward, or public-spirited citizens who wished to see the guilty punished for their offences. It was in the public interest that nothing should be done which was likely to discourage persons of either class from coming forward.
>
> (*R. v Rankine*, before Lord Chief Justice Lane,
> Law Report, *The Times*, 4 March 1986)

That encouragement could be in various forms, one of which was the prospect of reduction in sentence. Lord Justice Bingham listed the rewards:

> It was particularly important that persons concerned with the importation of drugs into the U.K. should be encouraged by the sentencing policy of the courts to give information to the police. An immediate confession of guilt, coupled with considerable assistance to the police could therefore be marked by a substantial reduction in what would otherwise be a proper sentence.
>
> (*R. v Afzal*, *The Times*, 14 October, 1989)

In this case a sentence of seven-and-half years was reduced to six years. There was not, however, an expectation of a reduction in sentence just because the offender was an informer. Reductions had to be related to index offences. In *R. v Preston and McAlery*, Mr Justice Farqarharson in the Court of Appeal, delivering the judgment of the court, said:

> What the courts should not take into account therefore as a result of this judgment is evidence of information given by an accused person which does not relate to the crime of which he now stands. The proper course to be taken was that where information is given by an accused person which does not relate to the crime of which he is charged, then that is a matter which the authorities can properly take into account, but it is not a matter for the court to consider in mitigation of the sentence passed.
>
> (*The Times*, 14 December 1987)

In order to operate a successful informer system the informer has to be protected, especially during the trial. One of the most important cases heard in Britain was *R. v Birtles* [1969] (53 Cr.App.Rep 469), where the court accepted that informers should be protected, at least within certain limits. The court recognised that such decisions may be disagreeable, but it thought the police should be allowed to make the best use of their informers. For practitioners this was a turning-point. That year also saw the introduction of the Home Office Guidelines on informers, which was the first time in Britain that formal documentary advice had been provided (Home Office, 1969).

The decision taken in *Birtles* to protect the informer at his trial, almost at all costs, continued for at least another decade. However, a Law Report in the *Daily Telegraph* (11 September 1989) pointed to a growing unease that defendants were now being denied the opportunity to prove their innocence.

> There was overwhelming public interest in keeping secret the source of information but… there was even stronger public interest in allowing a defendant to put forward a tenable case in the best light.
>
> (*Daily Telegraph*, 11 September 1989)

Demands by the defence that the informer be identified, and subject to open cross-examination, make the police less comfortable and the informers even more so. Requests to disclose the informer's identity, for this is what the defence was asking, led to a number of cases being withdrawn by the Crown Prosecution Service (CPS). Offering no evidence rather than proceeding with the prosecution may be regarded as morally wrong, but the fear that informers were being compromised and exposed to danger was also real. In 1993, for example, the Regional Crime Squad reported that three informers had been murdered in the previous twelve months (see Billingsley, 2000). The net effect is that more cases are now being withdrawn and more criminals are going free.

In English law there is no defence of entrapment but there is if an *agent provocateur* leads to the commission of further offences. Entrapment exists where an offence has been engineered by a law enforcement officer or his agent, in other words an informer. In effect, entrapment means the offence has been committed which would not otherwise have occurred had it not been for the actions of the police (*ibid*). The courts do not condone such actions, and they require the use made of informers to be kept within strict limits, otherwise they fear grave injustices may result; but they do not condemn them out of hand. The judgment of Lord Parker, referring to the case of *R. v Macro* sets out the position.

> It is vitally important to ensure as far as possible that the informer does not create an offence, that is to say incite others to commit an offence, which those others would not otherwise have committed. It is one thing for the police to make use of information concerning an offence that is already laid on... and to that end it may be perfectly proper for them to encourage the informer to take part in the offence, or indeed for the police officer himself to do so. But it is quite another thing, and something of which the court thoroughly disapproves, to use an informer to encourage another to commit an offence, or indeed an offence of a more serious nature, which he would not otherwise commit, still more so if the police themselves take part in carrying it out.
>
> (quoted in Khan and Gillance, 1976: 537)

The term 'laid on' is the critical one: if the offence was already 'laid on' then police participation to bring an offender to justice would be acceptable, at least within defined limits. If not, then the evidence would be unacceptable. Finding the correct balance will always be difficult (*ibid*: 538); for example it may be acceptable for an undercover agent to bring drugs to Britain in order that overseas drug dealers could be arrested, but it may not be acceptable for an informer to bring drugs into Britain to sell them to dealers. In the first case the court ordered the informer to be identified, and the case was abandoned; in the second, the appeal was dismissed, for 'if on occasion the big fish are lured here, then hooked, there is no abuse in that' (Marton, 1994, quoted in Billingsley, 2000).

Closely linked to entrapment is the *agent provocateur*, defined as 'a person who entices others to commit an express breach of the law which he would not otherwise have committed, and then proceeds or informs against him in respect of such an offence' (*Royal Commission on Police Powers and Procedures*, 1929, quoted in Khan and Gillance, 1976: 536). It all depends on the way the evidence was obtained and the extent to which informers create an offence. A fear was expressed in the 1970s that informers were being used to set up crimes, recruit participants and give evidence against them. If this was so, then three main questions should be asked:

(a)  how much can the police participate in an offence?

(b)  how much can they resort to trickery?, and

(c)  how far can they breach the law themselves?

McLean argued that an informer's evidence could be used in corroboration with that of the police. This produced a swift retort from *Liberty*, the civil liberties organisation, which said: 'We do not think it is the job of the police to go round committing crime. We think it is their job to prevent crime. To step over the line is a breach of their role' (quoted in Billingsley, 2000).

There the matter rests, or at least it rests until the next important legal judgment. However, in May 1969 the Home Office issued a Circular to Chief Officers of Police setting out the principles to be followed where the police make use of informers. These are as follows:

1    If society is to be protected from criminals the police must be able to make use of informers in appropriate circumstances, and within limits should be protected.

2    Strict limits should be imposed on the extent of an informer's participation in a crime.

3    No member of the police and no informer should counsel incite or procure the commission of a crime.

4    The police must not embark on a course which will constrain them to withhold information from or mislead a court in order to protect an informer.

5    There must be effective supervision by senior and experienced officers in the use of informers, and particular care must be given to the training of detectives in the subject (quoted in Khan and Gillance, 1976: 537).

How far and to what extent the Circular remains appropriate is a matter which will be examined throughout this book. The point to be made here is a different one: it is that changes are taking place in the nature of criminality. It is now international, dominated by drug money, where the key players rarely live in the countries in which the offences are committed. English law will have to consider these changes: entrapment, use of *agent provocateurs* and the judgments surrounding them will not easily bring the modern offender to justice unless these changes in the pattern of criminality are recognised. The trick is to do what has always been done, but in a different form: to prosecute the offender without compromising traditional civil liberties, and as always that will be no easy task.

## Handling informers

Recognition by the government of the need to control informers has been slow, and only recently has there been a concerted attempt to regulate their use, and that of the police officer who is the designated handler. One wonders whether the reluctance to provide guidelines has something to do with a wish not to state publicly that informers are being used in unsavoury ways. However in 1969, after a number of legal cases where the use of informers had been criticised, the then Home Secretary said:

> If society is to be protected from criminals the police must be able to make use of informants in appropriate circumstances. Informants appropriately employed are essential to criminal investigation, and within limits ought to be protected.
>
> (quoted in Billingsley, 2000)

Guidelines were introduced in May 1969 by a Home Office Circular (Home Office, 97/1969) and these have remained in operation. Briefly, as stated earlier, the Guidelines stipulated that no one should incite the commission of an offence, or act as *agent provocateur*. Informers may be allowed to participate in crime, but only where certain conditions apply, and police officers must not mislead the court; nor can police officers offer immunity if the informer continues to commit crime against their advice. The police can make payments from public funds if supervised.

In 1992 the police were beginning to express concern that the Home Office Circular needed to be updated. The Association of Chief Police Officers (ACPO) examined the use and management of informers and concluded that 'the effective handling and exploitation of information calls for judgement, experience and the management of risk'. The question was and still is, has the use of informers been given adequate attention? Are the risks understood, and is there an appropriate organisation to control the informers? John Grieve argues that the root of all problems with informers is the weakness of the officers involved, and the failure of the organisation to outline the dangers. He goes on to say that unless management systems are properly in place 'the informer will become more prolific, a more dangerous criminal than those we are seeking to destroy' (quoted in Billingsley, 2000).

The aim must be to find that delicate balance where handlers are not stifled by the inflexibility of controls, but equally not allowed to operate in ways which allow corruption to flourish. John Grieve again:

> The relationship between the informant and his handler is a hot-house where corruption can flourish. You have to have a system. It has to be open to audit analysts and third-party scrutiny
>
> (quoted in Billingsley, 2000)

John Grieve insists that handling informers requires skill and integrity backed by strong management and clear guidelines. It places demands on the police to manage and operate under a measure of risk and in conditions of uncertainty. The situation remains tenable as long as the decision-making process is open to scrutiny, where the records are complete and where an outside body could, if it so wishes, carry out a comprehensive audit. Producing a workable solution is the challenge ahead for the police and others – including the informers themselves.

## The Human Rights Act 1998

Throughout this volume there are numerous references to the Human Rights Act 1998, with observations about its importance and relevance to the use of informers. The Act became law in Britain in October 2000, and will clearly have an impact on policy and practice. Here, we can only give a broad outline of some of the main features as they affect informers, and speculate about some of its likely effects.

The Act arose out of the European Convention on Human Rights (ECHR), which aims to 'to protect the fundamental rights and freedoms of all'. The Convention itself is not new and had earlier been debated in Parliament and elsewhere. Nonetheless, the Human Rights Act 1998 will integrate that Convention into English law. It will also create a statutory requirement for all legislation, past, present and future, to be made compatible with the Convention; that is to say all legislation will have to be interpreted accordingly. Where disputes arise, and no satisfactory conclusion can be reached, the case will then go to the European Court in Strasbourg. All member states have been given a measure of freedom to ensure their own public policies are given due consideration; this is known as the 'margin of appreciation'.

For these purposes the most relevant sections are Article 6, which gives the right to a fair trial, and Article 8, which grants the right to privacy. Article 6 is a complex section and as far as informers are concerned will produce conflict with English law. For example, Article 6 will give informers the right to remain silent – a proposition which lies at the heart of the Human Rights Act. In Britain no such right exists; more than that, a court in England and Wales can take account of, and draw inferences when defendants remain silent. Moreover, Article 6 is concerned with the way the evidence is obtained, placing a duty on prosecutors to disclose relevant facts to the court, presumably including the name of the informer. In Britain protecting the informer's identity is regarded as necessary if informers are to be encouraged to come forward and provide information to the police, although increasingly it is becoming more common for the defence to ask that the informers identity be disclosed.

Article 8 grants the right to privacy in family life, home and correspondence, and prohibits intervention by any public authority unless it is necessary. Again, ECHR will be in conflict with British practices, especially as it affects the use of covert policing, for covert policing clearly violates Article 8 as, by its very nature its intention is to undermine the right to privacy for those subject to its practices. Moreover, there is the problem of how that special group of informers, the participating informers, are to remain operational. Participating informers by definition continue to commit offences, albeit under supervision and by permission of their controllers. Interestingly enough, the Home Office no longer wants to call them 'participating informers', presumably because that appears to be condoning criminality; it prefers the term 'covert human intelligence sources' instead.

Nonetheless, participating informers, or whatever they are to be called, are too important to be jettisoned, and ways need to be found to retain them. The solution for this and other measures has been to introduce new legislation, in this case the Regulation of Investigatory Powers Act, still before Parliament, to permit law enforcement agencies to contravene relevant aspects of ECHR. For Article 8, that means that the use of intrusive surveillance is to be accepted, if the police are satisfied that certain conditions have been met. These are that it is 'necessary, and proportionate', and the police are sure that the intrusion is directed against the target, and not at some innocent bystander.

There appears to be little in the way of European case law to assist the debate. Cases will doubtless centre on the need for the prosecution to establish whether the informer should be allowed to commit the type of crime under investigation. Simply stated, the court will have to distinguish between creating an opportunity to commit an offence, which it regards as acceptable, and inducing the commission of an offence which it regards as not.

At the time of writing (September 2000) it is still not clear whether the new Regulation of Investigatory Powers Act will achieve its objectives, including the provision of a basis in law for the deployment of participating informers. The general expectation is that it will, and also allow police forces to use informers, participating or not, justified on the basis that 'in a democratic society in the interests of national security, public safety, or the economic well-being of the country for the prevention of crime, for the protection of health or morals, or for the protection of the rights and freedom of others'.   With effect from 2 October 2000 every public authority, which includes police forces, must ensure that their day-to-day work is compatible with the Human Rights Act. A police force or other public authority found to be in breach of that Act will not, however, be subject to criminal proceedings, but there would be a civil remedy. That could include granting the victim, depending on the circumstances of the case, an award of damages, compensation, and/or having the original verdict quashed. Clearly, for the police, or any other authority found not complying with the law the financial implications are huge. It will be some time before a body of case law develops, providing some clarity about how and under what circumstances informers can be used. In the meantime the police must cope as best they can with what will be a new dimension to their work.

## An introduction to the chapters in this book

We suggested earlier that the police often become uneasy when outsiders ask questions about informers, sometimes with some justification. The problem for the police, however, is that the more they build barriers against those who would ask questions, the more outsiders suspect something may be amiss. There are, after all, legitimate questions to ask, which can be answered in ways that do not threaten the integrity of the system, or present a danger to those working within it.

The fact that this is one of the first books written on informers, with some chapters written by serving police officers, perhaps refects a new openness within the police force. Conducting research does not mean exposing those working in the system to additional risk, nor operating in ways resembling investigative journalists, eager to expose every defect to the outside world. It means asking legitimate questions about the effectiveness of the system, its cost, and the ethics of its mode of operation, amongst other things. So, for example, it is reasonable to ask to what extent the informer system reduces crime, or to what extent it makes it worse? (If the health services can be accused of producing iatrogenic disorders and ill-health, and the universities of producing ignorance, so fundamental questions can be asked of those involved in crime control). Or, how much does the system cost, and is it cost effective? What ethical questions are raised by the use of informers, and how best to deal with them? And what sort of system is required to encourage informers, which on the one hand protects them yet on the other produces a measure of openness, allowing third party scrutiny? These are not the only questions to be asked by any means, but they are, in our view some of the most important, and we have tried to answer them here.

In *chapter 1* Philip Bean and Roger Billingsley ask some of these basic questions, concentrating on the effectiveness of informers in reducing crime. They do so by examining the use of informers in drug markets where claims by some dealers that others have 'a licence to deal' are commonplace. Drug markets place the problems of the participating informer into sharp relief, for while allowing dealers to continue dealing may be one way to obtain information on other dealers, it may also promote and exacerbate the drug problem. The authors show that there are procedures adopted by the police, sometimes as a response to Government demands, which also make matters worse, in particular the use of performance indicators where the police are required to deal with certain types of criminality, such as, burglary, without considering that it may be drug-driven. They may arrest burglars but ignore the drug market which sustains them. Drugs, and the problems they bring are referred to throughout this volume; this chapter highlights some of the persistent problems which stem from drug markets.

One such problem is police corruption, dealt with by Roy Clark in *chapter 2*. The link between drugs and police corruption is such that were there to be a question as to where resources should be directed for anti-corruption work, the obvious place to begin would be where there are informers, where they are handled, and where there are drugs. Drugs, informers and corruption go hand in hand: the drugs and the money are readily available with the informer almost certainly having access to both

Roy Clark argues on the one hand for the continued use of informers for intelligence-led policing, but recognises that informers pose the greatest danger to police integrity. He shows that where standards have fallen this is almost always due to a mixture of structural and personal defects, for example a lack of supervision, leading officers to becoming vulnerable to temptation. This chapter centres on a case study in the Metropolitan District involving the corrupt practices of a serving police officer who subsequently received a sentence of eleven years' imprisonment. This case is remarkable in a number of respects, not least in that it shows how corrupt officers experience a complete role reversal, the criminal becomes the handler and the corrupt officer becomes the informer, with all the loss of status and respect that entails. Roy Clark shows how this role reversal is a common trait with corrupt officers. He shows too how corrupt officers lose respect and credibility amongst those who undertake the corrupting. Corruption produces role reversal; that much is clear with the paradox all too evident. The final ironical twist is that when the corrupt police officer is detected it is likely to be the erstwhile informer who informs on him.

In *chapter 3* Tom Williamson and Peter Bagshaw address some of the ethical issues surrounding the use of informers by law enforcement agencies. They ask whether the police can justify, ethically, such use, especially after such high profile cases as that of Stephen Lawrence in which informers were actively involved. They also raise the matter of police corruption and like Roy Clark note that corruption is closely associated with the use of informers. They identify two types of corruption, so-called 'process' corruption and 'noble cause' corruption. The former occurs where the police falsify and violate procedures to secure a conviction, believing that the offender is guilty anyway; the latter occurs where convictions are falsely secured for some supposedly higher cause, such as providing society with a respite from a particular offender. Tom Williamson and Peter Bagshaw say of the latter that the officers involved are misguided rather than evil, and that the solution lies in more appropriate supervision. They want the whole police culture to be reviewed, not just in relation to the use of informers. They cite as an example of good practice how one police force has created professional standards guidance to alleviate some of the problems. Finally, they consider the question of whether the use of informers can ever be ethical. They find some ethical justification on utilitarian grounds, but make the point that the available research, albeit limited, has failed to support the notion that informers are cost effective and efficient. They want greater use of ethics committees to assist the police in the way informers are used.

Nigel South in *chapter 4* discusses accountability in the use of informers. He compares police informers with security service informers where, although the security services are not enforcement agencies they nonetheless have objectives which are similar – to infiltrate organisations and gather information. Nigel South makes the point that if the police and Security Services are allowed to employ covert and intrusive methods of surveillance, including the use of informers, there must be appropriate mechanisms to make them accountable. The new National Guidelines referred to throughout this book will provide, he believes, some necessary reassurance, but considers a major criticism of current practice to be the use of coercion to obtain information.

Practitioners of course argue that whilst the use of informers is often unpalatable, they are effective as a means of clearing up crime. Nigel South is unconvinced. Firstly, he says information is not always acted upon; secondly, lower-grade information is rarely given the necessary priority; thirdly, most crimes are cleared up as a result of information from the public; and finally, many detectives argue that they can be equally successful without using informers. Accountability is seen as the key, and this means establishing a balance between the need for openness and the need to protect the informer's identity, especially in court. The efficiency of informers and the need for secrecy are part of a tension which is evident in many of the chapters of this book.

A reoccurring question also has been about the motives of informers. So what satisfactions do informers obtain, and why do they inform when often the rewards are so poor? In *chapter 5* Roger Billingsley examines the motives of informers, using data from his own research. Hitherto there has been much speculation but little hard data on what these motives are. Skolnick, quoting Harney and Cross, lists seven main motives for informing and provides a case in point. The first motive is said to be fear, primarily of the law, but presumably too because of the possibility of receiving a long sentence. The second motive is revenge. A third they call 'perverse' but which hardly seems perverse, for it involves informing on the illegal activities of a competitor, and is a common activity amongst drug dealers. A fourth motive is that informers take pleasure in informing, and a fifth is because they are 'demented, eccentric or a nuisance'. A sixth is financial gain, and finally there are those who inform because they are repentant – 'not frequently seen but they may be valuable' (quoted in Skolnick, 1967: 123).

Other typologies can and have been developed which to a greater or lesser extent include the list given above. Rarely are they based on empirical data and equally rarely is there any suggestion that motives may change. Roger Billingsley is able to show that they do; for example, some may begin because of financial rewards but continue because they enjoy their involvement with the police, or some may begin for revenge but later enjoy the financial rewards.

This research has important implications, especially for practitioners. The relationship between informer and handler is integral to its success, but without a clear understanding of the informer's motives the relationship may be less efficient and effective than it should be. Roger Billingsley argues that the handler, and management too for that matter, must be aware of the informer's reasons for giving information if the relationship is to remain secure and of advantage to the police. He shows how the most valuable informers are those who begin by taking pleasure from informing, probably enjoying the power they have, and become more professional and mercenary over time. In some cases public funds might well be paid unnecessarily – presumably some informers who take pleasure from informing would inform for less – but their motivational change will produce a different set of circumstances which the handler must consider if the relationship is to be profitable.

Given role differences relating to gender it is reasonable to expect variations in motives and methods between male and female informers. But how and in what way? In *chapter 6* Teresa Nemitz shows that fewer women become informers and proportionately fewer women police officers become handlers. However, when they do they lack the need to display the 'macho' image, being more content to listen rather than dictate terms. Their motives for being informers are more likely to be bound up with the preservation of their family (not always the case, of course), and if they become protected witnesses they find relocation difficult if it means being separated from earlier family networks. As resident informers serving a prison sentence, women will serve it in a designated police station as there are no units in women's prisons.

However, it seems that one of the main reasons why more women are seeking witness protection arises out of domestic violence. More women appear to be coming forward to give evidence against partners involved in serious crime in order to protect themselves and possibly their children from physical abuse and rape. Giving evidence places them and their children in danger. Witness protection schemes offer security but they can also lead to relocation to another part of the country or abroad, and taking on new identities for everyone, including the children. The decision to inform on their partners is likely to be an act of last resort in the face of desperation.

Teresa Nemitz also shows that the female handlers' perceptions of informers differed from their male colleagues. Female handlers agreed that the best informers – meaning those that gave the most credible information – come from members of the community, male and female, rather than the criminal world. Women handlers often criticised the male handler's macho views of informers – the armed robber, the Mr Big in the drug world, or the male view that informers have to be 'good criminals'. Teresa Nemitz concludes that the gender issues raised in this chapter, which highlight interesting differences between female informers and handlers and the special problems of women seeking witness protection, call for concerted effort for more research.

Paul Iganski and Carole Ballardie, in *chapter 7*, are concerned with the thorny question of the use of juvenile informers and the ethical and practical problems they create. A large amount of petty crime, including theft, is committed by juveniles; the peak age of crime after all is 15 years and the peak age group 15–18 years, so it is perhaps reasonable to assume that juveniles will be recruited as informers, at least on a *pro rata* basis. To do so of course raises a number of ethical and operational questions; for example should a juvenile be asked to inform against his/her parents, or how can a young drug offender be rehabilitated if the police encourage association with other users in order to obtain information? Some police forces do not use juvenile informers, and there would be many outside the police service who would agree with this line. Nonetheless they are used, and they are useful because they can and do provide important information, perhaps being the only possible sources of information on certain types of crime, and certain highly specific family situations. However, as Paul Iganski and Carole Ballardie show, there exist considerable disparities in the use of juveniles throughout the criminal justice system, not just as an informer but as witness, offender, and victim.

Yet juveniles are citizens too and should have comparable rights with adults, whilst at the same time being recognised as being impressionable and vulnerable. That is the essential dilemma.

Most police forces show care when it comes to using juveniles as informers and accept that appropriate structures need to be in place if juveniles are to be given the necessary protection and care. Even so, and however robust these structures are, they can only provide physical protection; moral protection is more difficult. That is what makes the use of juveniles as informers such a minefield in which to work.

Steven Greer in *chapter 8* discusses the role of the supergrass. Supergrasses are those professional criminals who decide to give information against other criminals, often their associates, hoping thereby to secure a reduced sentence for themselves. Supergrasses inform on a number of offenders and the offences about which they give information are usually the most serious, including terrorism. There were a number of trials in 1972 when the use of the term 'supergrass' was used, especially in Northern Ireland, and the Royal Ulster Constabulary were claiming the system was having a devastating effect on terrorism. At the same time it was also arousing controversy. Some critics saw it as creating 'internment by remand' by keeping alleged offenders in prison and delaying their trial; others saw it as not cost-effective. For example, supergrasses, whether they were terrorists or not tended to require long-term protection, involving high running costs and long-term and extensive financial assistance. They also tended to re-offend and cause embarrassment to the authorities. If the supergrass is to continue to give evidence that evidence must be properly corroborated, otherwise the danger is that supergrasses will fabricate evidence to receive a better deal from the court.

This wide-ranging chapter compares the use of supergrasses in England and Wales, the US, Italy, Northern Ireland and Germany, showing how the American system, with its links to witness protection schemes differed initially (but less so now) from those elsewhere. A central theme relates to the types of crimes about which supergrasses inform – that is, organised crime and political violence. Steven Greer also examines the process that began after the collapse of the Berlin wall in 1989 when members of the Stasi (the East German secret police) were offered reduced sentences in return for becoming 'State witnesses'; and how Spanish and French anti-terrorist legislation sought to encourage members of terrorist organisations to inform on their colleagues. Steven Greer concludes his chapter with a discussion of the anti-terrorist process that was put in place after the Maro assassination in Italy, and the informer evidence central to the trials of right- and left-wing terrorists in Germany in the 1980s and 1990s.

Central to Steven Greer's argument is that there have been major criticisms of supergrasses wherever supergrass trials have taken place.

There have been serious doubts about the credibility of the information coming from known offenders, and of convictions gained from the testimony of supergrasses without corroboration – and the legitimacy of the criminal justice system dealing with criminals.

*Chapter 9* is about Crimestoppers and the way it has developed over the last decade or so. Crimestoppers is a community informer system, appealing to those who seek anonymity yet want to provide the police with information. Bill Griffiths and Alan Murphy describe it as a prime source of intelligence in that it captures information that would not otherwise be available, whilst guaranteeing freedom from intimidation. Not surprisingly, Crimestoppers encourages those who supply information to continue to do so, and encourages some to become a registered informer handled by an officer outside the Crimestoppers unit. Over the years the numbers of these informers has increased steadily.

The results from Crimestoppers are impressive. The data presented by Bill Griffiths and Alan Murphy show how information has led to the arrest of serious offenders, including those for murder, attempted murder, rape, firearms offences, robbery and burglary, together with a large number of drug dealers. Of course not all information supplied to Crimestoppers is of that order; some is of little or no value but a great deal is, and seen as crucial to subsequent detection. The authors conclude that Crimestoppers provides a significant benefit to law enforcement, including Customs and Excise (who receive the same information), by producing results that would not be secured otherwise, working in partnership with the community. Crimestoppers can only operate and flourish with public support, and that it clearly does shows it is the model community informer system.

In *chapter 10* Philip Bean looks at witness protection schemes. Not all informers require witness protection and not all those on witness protection are informers, but some are and they come through different routes (Maynard, 2000). There are the participating informers whose identity has been compromised whilst remaining active informers, or they may have been arrested alongside those on whom they were informing. Then there are those recruited as informers after arrest who may perhaps be seeking a lighter sentence. Informers, alongside all others, will only be accepted onto the witness protection programme if they are in serious danger, and only then after a thorough risk assessment.

Entry into the programme can lead to a change of identity, including that for the whole family, and may lead to a new address which may be in another country.

For some informers witness protection is a long-term affair, where any return to the old way of life, which usually means a return to committing offences, will be a dangerous matter. They must also expect to be taken off the witness protection scheme should they return to their old haunts; those running the scheme are likely to be told of this by other informers. If they receive a prison sentence they will serve it in separate institutions alongside other informers on protection, and on discharge enter the same scheme as others. Clearly, at this level witness protection can remain successful only by guaranteeing the safety of each witness, and is an expensive and time-consuming exercise. It is a sign of the times that informers must take their place alongside others, like police officers and judges, who also require protection.

A study of informers would not be complete without attention given to the Human Rights Act 1998 which came into operation in October 2000. Peter Neyroud and Alan Beckley address this in *chapter 11*. They provide an examination of the way this Act and the Regulation of Investigatory Powers Act 2000 (or RIPA) is to operate. RIPA is the British Government's response to the Human Rights Act, which requires that law enforcement operations are looked at from the viewpoint of the citizen not the law enforcement agencies. Hence interference with the citizen's right to 'private and family life' through a deceptive relationship with an informer will require a clear legal basis, whether or not the interference results in a subsequent court case. RIPA provides a statutory regime for policing which not only meets the demands of the Human Rights Act but a clear legal basis for areas of policing not previously governed by statute. This chapter describes the main provisions of RIPA, and the way its framework has been constituted, with special attention given to the new concept of covert human intelligence sources (CHIS), another term for informers.

## Some concluding comments

A book such as this can only cover a small part of what is an extensive and developing subject. We believe we have only scratched the surface of an area of policing that has remained hidden for too long, and without outside influence. We know that there is much to learn from the practitioners about informers, but suspect that practitioners will benefit from a more open discussion about what they do and how they go about things. As we say throughout, this is one of the first books on informers and we hope it may set the pattern for others.

The topics selected are to a large extent related to the editors' own interests, but equally are related to the expertise of those with experience in the handling of informers. This volume has tended to concentrate on ethical questions rather than practical aspects, and on the British experience rather than taking an international perspective. In some areas there are gaps in empirical data, but the reasons for that are obvious; with one or two exceptions no empirical studies exist. That alone ought to be the main priority for the immediate future, and the aim should be to produce methodologically sound studies looking at relatively basic features of the informer system, asking questions about who does what, to whom and how? Answering some of the questions posed throughout this volume would be an impressive start to a research-based study of informers.

This is not to say that legal jurisprudential or ethical questions should be ignored – there are plenty of those waiting to be answered. The impact of ECHR needs close examination, alongside a constant scrutiny of national and local guidelines and their operation. The position of juvenile informers produces intractable ethical dilemmas, particularly when the juveniles are known drug users and their rewards used to sustain a habit. Can it ever be right to encourage family members to inform on others, juvenile or not, and if so at what point does the end justify those means? There is something ethically unsavoury about the whole informer system, but presumably less so when it produces results which would not otherwise be achieved. And what impact does this have on those working the system? To be involved in measures of deceit, particularly as an undercover agent, may have anti-therapeutic consequences which require closer attention, and are no doubt the price some officers pay for their involvement.

Other questions need attention. We have concentrated in this book on policing using the term in its traditional sense. Agencies including Customs and Excise, the Immigration Service, the Security Services, and even the Inland Revenue rely on and use informers. How different are their practices and to what extent are they effective in achieving their aims? These are some of the questions we need to consider, and do so in a way which does not jeopardise the safety of those working within the system, but which does permit a more open debate.

# References

Bean, P. T. (1992) *Cocaine and Crack in Nottingham. A follow-up study*. Unpublished report to the Home Office.

Billingsley, R. (2000) 'An examination of the relationship between informers and their handlers within the police service in England'. Unpublished Ph.D. thesis, Loughborough University.

Campbell, D. (1991) 'Whisper who dares', *Police Review*, 15 March: 532–533.

Colvin M. (2000) 'Bill makes complex legal environment yet more so'. *Times*, 29 February.

*Daily Telegraph* Law Reports, 11 September 1989.

Dorn, N., Murji, K. and South, N. *et al* (1992) *Traffickers: drug markets and law enforcement*, London: Routledge.

Dunnighan, C. (1992) 'Reliable sources', *Police Review*, 14 August: 1496–7.

Grieve, J. (1992) 'The police contribution to drugs education: a role for the 1990s', in Evans, R. and O'Connor, L., *Drug Abuse and Misuse: developing educational strategies in partnership*, Fulton: 53–64.

Home Office (1969) *Informants who take part in crime*. Home Office Circular 97/1969, 12 May.

Khan, A. and Gilliance, K. (1976) 'Agent Provocateur', *Police Review*, 30 April: 536–8.

Maynard, W. (1994) *Witness Intimidation. Strategies for Prevention*, Police Research Group. Home Office, Paper 55.

Skolnick, J. (1967) *Justice without Trial*, New York: Wiley.

*The Times* Law Reports, *R. v Rankine* before Lord Chief Justice and Lord Lane, 4 March 1986; *R. v Anthony Garner*; *R. v Preston and McAlery*, and *R. v Afzel*, 14 October 1989.

# 1 Drugs, crime and informers

## Philip Bean and Roger Billingsley

Informers, as all law enforcement agencies keep telling us, are central to policing, and especially in the drugs field. In respect of the USA, Jerome Skolnick reminds us that whilst the police can arrest drug users by cruising in unmarked cars looking for those tell-tale signs of dealing, the apprehension of one small-time drug dealer does not constitute a 'good bust' (Skolnick, 1967: 120-1). The drug squad detective wants the leading figure in the supply system, a 'Mr Big', and for that to happen some level of organisational penetration is necessary. Skolnick sees informers as a favoured method of promoting that 'bust'.

For this and other reasons policing the drugs field would be almost impossible without informers. Drug misuse is a victimless crime; the drug purchaser is unlikely to complain about his supplier. Fortunately, at least from the perspective of the police, informers are generous with their information, whether of the types of drugs, of the structure of the organisation, or of the personnel who maintain it. John Grieve says from his experience as a police officer there is no shortage of information, or of informers. The problem for the police is to find ways to handle it.

> If there is one thing true about the drug scene it is that it is imbued with treachery. You will discover that far from being secretive people will talk to you all the time, that you will start asking questions and people will answer them, and tell you about what is going on. I have never met so many informers that a drug field generates when compared to other forms of crime.
>
> (Grieve, 1992: 58)

It is not just that the drug world is 'imbued with treachery', though that may be so; it is that addict populations, especially if they are street addicts, consume large quantities of heroin, are invariably unstable, and almost certainly heavily involved in criminal activity. Supporting a large drug habit requires ingenuity plus an ability to know where to acquire and sell stolen goods. During periods of withdrawal the drug user's instability takes a more hyperbolic form; they will do and say almost anything for the next 'fix', including giving information to the police about their competitors. Similarly, whilst under the influence of drugs they may have long since forgotten where the truth begins or ends. Handling this type of informer is a difficult business, yet paradoxically the best informers are the unstable, for they are well acquainted with the drug trade and deeply involved in criminal activity. They may also hold influential positions in the supply system.

The question we want to ask here is: what impact do informers have on the overall nature of the drug problem? Or put differently, does the use of informers reduce the level of drug use and drug-related crimes, or does it increase it? We also want to ask about current police practices and about the direction they are likely to take. We think these are interesting and important questions given the way the supply system operates, with implications far beyond that of the drug user, and extending to and including other areas of crime.

## Licence to deal

In 1992, whilst undertaking a study of crack/cocaine use in Nottingham, one of us (PB) received complaints from dealers that others had 'a licence to deal'. They meant that some dealers appeared to enjoy a favoured relationship with the police, who in return for information allowed the so-called 'licenced' dealers to continue with immunity. The police of course denied they issued 'licences', but the term was used so often as to lead us to suspect that something of this nature was occurring. These 'licences' were said to be have been given in a variety of circumstances. For example, it was believed that certain clubs were never raided, or that certain houses were allowed to sell crack/cocaine without being 'busted'. As one dealer said: 'We had been encouraged by the Drug Squad to be used as a "crack house" for a three-year period. They offered us police protection but that disappeared when we stopped singing.'

There may of course be good reasons why the police did not raid those clubs which had nothing to do with granting 'licences' or otherwise – for example, inertia, or lack of resources. However, local residents reacted with horror at what they saw as the unimpeded growth of a local 'crack house' in their residential area. It was not just the disruption drug dealers created, and the corresponding threatening atmosphere, but a sense of confusion about police intentions. Some residents questioned whether crack use in Nottingham would have ever reached the level it did were it not for the drug squad and their policies towards informers.

Jerome Skolnick recognises that reports about 'licences' are not entirely without foundation but he says they are exaggerated. He says reports persist because those without 'licences' and those betrayed by informers feel the rewards given by their betrayers were higher than they actually were. 'Typically the betrayed cannot bring themselves to believe how little they have been sold out for.' (Skolnick, 1967: 126). Dorn, Murji and South would not agree, and talk of informers who continue to deal with the knowledge of the police – becoming what are technically called participating informers. They go on to say, 'By selling relatively small amounts but making oneself available as one may later be able to supply much bigger amounts, trafficker informants put themselves in a position of being approached by other traffickers who wish to obtain large amounts.' (Dorn, Murji, and South, 1992: 143-4).

The police recognise this, or rather acknowledge that their informers might continue to ply their trade, but a small-time dealer has the perfect cover to enable him to know what is going on, and may even know the larger dealers in the area. If 'Mr Big' is the ultimate prize 'licenced' dealers provide the best way forward.

The suspicions and accusations surrounding the so-called 'licenced' dealers extend far beyond providing immunity from prosecution. Some dealers, who were known as police informers, were, we were told, planted by higher level dealers, and their privileged position used by these higher level dealers to their advantage. That is, they were to learn of police operations, giving those higher level dealers insider knowledge of police tactics. Or, in another case we were told that informer dealers were encouraged to continue informing by other dealers so that they could also use their premises. Of course, the informer dealers had to restrict his information if they were to protect those who were using them to extend their activities.

Data on 'licences' was difficult to obtain and that which was available was mainly anecdotal, creating more of a set of tentative hypotheses than anything else. If 'licences' exist, as we strongly suspect they do, their impact needs to be studied, let alone their legitimacy. Obtaining that data will not be easy, but if one of the questions to be answered is to establish the effect of informers on police prosecutions, and crime levels generally, then the data becomes a necessary part of any detailed examination. If, as we suspect, something of this sort exists, then it is hypothesized that they increase the level and extent of dealing and help promote drug use amongst those who have not yet established a habit; it is after all those who are less sophisticated in the ways of drug markets who are drawn to these street-level dealers. All such dealing and drug use has to be offset by the arrest of higher level dealers. Even so, we suspect that the extent of use will be the greater and more than outweigh the advantages where 'licences' are provided.

## The effectiveness of the drug informer

One of the questions we wish to explore is the extent to which informers are effective. A great deal is made of the way informers are used by the law enforcement agencies, and the accepted view is that they are a necessary, if regrettable, feature of modern policing. This may well be so, but how effective are they? We have already indicated that participating informers with or without their 'licences' to deal continue to commit offences and whilst doing so may make the situation worse. In other words, success obtained through informers must be offset by the offences committed by them. Clearly then, at this rather crude level things are not straightforward.

In technical terms measuring the effectiveness of drug informers involves determining what is called the absolute prosecution rate, or APR. The spontaneous prosecution rate, the SPR, and the participating informer rate, the PIR, offset this APR. That is to say, the total number of offenders prosecuted must be set against those who would have been prosecuted anyway (what we can call the spontaneous prosecution rate or SPR), together with those who were allowed to continue committing offences (what we can call the participating informer rate, or PIR). To find the absolute prosecution rate, or APR, the SPR and PIR must be subtracted from those prosecuted as a result of using informers. The APR is likely to be difficult to compute because the SPR is almost impossible to determine, leaving at best the possibility of a close approximation of the true figure.

In practice a less sophisticated measure of effectiveness can be undertaken using a number of different criteria. First, effectiveness can be calculated by the number of prosecutions the informer helps produce; this assumes that prosecution is the objective rather than disruption or obtaining intelligence. This is a relatively crude measure but valid nonetheless for it shows the strength of the informer's activities. So, for example, if the informer system brings in a number of prosecutions, perhaps more than would otherwise be expected the system can said to be effective. This method does not of course take account of those who would have been prosecuted anyway, the SPR, nor of the PIR but it provides some measure of effectiveness, however weak.

A second measure is concerned with the quality of the prosecutions; that is where informers produce higher levels of offenders than would have been the case otherwise. Again, the same defects arise as in the example above, with the same advantages. A third measure is to count the amount paid in rewards and set these against the value of items recovered while acting on information from informers. This method was suggested by the Metropolitan Police (1998) but has rather more defects than those above, and is hardly realistic when considering informing on (say) paedophiles or other victimless crimes; in this respect it is interesting that the Metropolitan Police Informant Working Group has recommended that there should be regular monitoring of the informer system, and wants a further study to consider how cost effectiveness can be measured (Metropolitan Police Informant Working Group, 1998: 9).

Finally, another method of establishing effectiveness is to concentrate on selected types of offenders who are rarely prosecuted because of the difficulties involved in getting information on them, and determine the part played by informers. An obvious example would be where the informer was instrumental in penetrating levels of organised crime which would not have been penetrated otherwise. This measure is often used by law enforcement agencies as a justification for informers, but it too suffers from the same defects as the methods above.

Notwithstanding the absence of hard data, or the lack of sophistication in measuring effectiveness, the general assumption remains that informers are invaluable and an important investigative tool. As one American commentator says,

> It is safe to say that 95 per cent of all Federal narcotics cases are obtained as a result of the work of informers. Narcotics agents… can uncover large syndicates selling narcotics only through informers and undercover agents who can 'tip' them off as peddlers and pushers. The latter in turn can lead agents to the wholesalers and importers.
>
> (Quoted in *Columbia Journal of Law and Social Problems*: 47)

Those favouring informers say that each case presents the possibility that informers will lead to deeper levels of penetration in a criminal organisation than hitherto, so that where the informers lead only to small-time dealers they are quickly dropped. They want to use large numbers of informers on the expectation that whilst the majority will not aid materially the goal of eradicating the organisation behind the trafficking some will, and they hope that an informer can go beyond the superficial level that sustains their belief in the system (*ibid*: 50). Their aim is to move beyond horizontal co-operation (where the informer produces successful prosecutions of so-called 'sidewalk' level dealers), to vertical co-operation which reaches higher level dealers and 'meaningful levels of crime' (*ibid*: 49). Informers become the *sina qua non* of any large police operation, and rather than see undercover agents as the major investigative officers, supporters of the use of informers regard them as the key to any penetration of illegal organisations. They say undercover officers can rarely do this on their own.

This view is not universally accepted, for there are those who argue that informers rarely lead to the successful prosecution of the 'Mr Bigs'. They believe that organised crime can only be stopped through extensive police work using undercover agents, and regard informers as superfluous. Critics point to the number of crimes committed by informers operating as so-called 'participating informers', for drug dealers must of necessity remain involved in the drug scene, and in practice this means they continue dealing. Critics say it means that the information provided is likely to be on other dealers operating at roughly similar levels, where it is reasonable to assume they inform to extend their own dealing network. It may be unfair to ascribe such motives to all informers at this level, but the police, sometimes from bitter experience, will know this is so. Leaving horizontal informers in the system usually leads to trouble. 'Too often informers make cases against individuals of less criminality who would not otherwise be involved. In fact informers increase the total crime in narcotics.' (*Columbia Journal of Law and Social Problems*: 47)

The case against the use of informers has been put in jurisprudential terms. Goldstein (1960, quoted in *ibid*: 55), an ardent critic of the use of informers, lists three reasons to be wary of them. First, he says police hesitancy to implicate an informer encourages others to be involved in crime; he talks of the manner in which the protected environment – what has earlier been called a licence to deal – cloaks not only the informer but those who operate alongside him, i.e. others dealing from the same premises. This, says Goldstein, encourages others to break the law. Second, Goldstein says informers are encouraged by the police to continue dealing and so maintain and actively expand their association with the underworld, where inevitably many become involved further in criminal activity. 'This result is especially undesirable in the case of first offenders since they are the most ripe for rehabilitation.' (*ibid*: 61). Thirdly, he says the practice can lead to widespread disrespect for the criminal justice system; that is to say, once informers believe that they can continue to commit offences all belief in the value of justice vanishes, especially that related to just deserts (*ibid*: 61).

This critique is sound in its jurisprudential arguments, and needs to be recognised and taken to heart – as it presumably has been by John Grieve when he says all informers should be 'busted' at least once a year to stop them getting out of control. The current trend, however, is to recruit more and more informers, especially in the drugs world where about thirty per cent of all informers used are thought to be drug informers. Dorn, Murji and South see the trend as being likely to continue, where the expanding field of drug use is likely to sweep up an increasing number of petty traffickers who will be induced to give information in return for promises of a lighter sentence (1992: 147). How to control these offenders, and meet Goldstein's critique, must be part of any study of effectiveness, and needs to be built into any evaluation.

## Modern policing, drug markets and informers

In the mid 1980s ACPO produced a policy for policing drug markets, the Broome Report (ACPO 1985, unpublished, but see Dorn, Murji and South: 1992). It offered a three-tier strategy. Tier 1, at the highest level was for the specialist police operators such as the National Crime Squad whose task was to deal with the top-level traffickers. Tier 2 was for the local drug squads and they were to deal with the local 'Mr Bigs', and Tier 3 was for the uniformed police officers who had to deal with local low-level street markets.

> 'First we must have a strategy of preventing importation and distribution and this must be done in conjunction with HM Customs. Secondly, Force drug squads must tackle drug distribution where it has evaded the first level of control. Finally, all officers at Divisional level should seek to remove drugs that reach street level.'
>
> (quoted in *ibid*: 210)

As a policy it was wrong in principle and damaging in practice. It was modelled on the supposed drug trafficking system which was thought to have three tiers, with the policing strategy designed to meet those tiers. The distribution system is not like that; the distribution system operates through a series of fluid networks rather than a unified structure. The other defect was that Divisional police rarely bothered to deal with street-level dealers, preferring to leave it to the drug squads, while the drug squads thought it beneath them to tackle small-time dealing. No one took ownership of the street-level dealers, and leaving them alone was a *de facto* way of legalising drug use. Fortunately, and not before time, the Broome strategy was discarded, to be replaced by a wide variety of methods, some of which we wish to consider here.

Following Broome, a major initiative was to set up drug wings for the regional crime squads, now the National Crime Squad. Their function was to concentrate on the major traffickers; they were staffed by police officers seconded from local forces and strategically based in the larger towns and cities. Their success was limited, but the main criticism came from those police forces that supplied the staff and consequently paid a share of the budget. They did not think they received an adequate return because there appeared to be no immediate relief from the drug problems in their area. Moreover, these crime squad officers lost touch with their informers, leading to a drop in local intelligence. In contrast, the crime squads argued that by attacking the sources of the problem in the major cities they would reduce availability. However, as only about ten per cent of the supply system is interrupted, and that mainly before it enters the country, this was a forlorn hope. There may be an argument in favour of crime squad officers having a more permanent secondment to the crime squads, but even that is contentious; however, this would at least give them the opportunity to cultivate informers.

A second initiative has been the development of the partnership approach, the emphasis being on the use of other agencies working together to solve a specific problem, for example, voluntary agencies, local authorities, the probation service. Low-level policing, for that is what partnerships are about, operates as a form of community policing, and works on the basis that no single agency can solve the crime problem, whereas multi-agency working may do so. Co-operation also helps agencies share resources, and produces a so-called value added approach, achieving a result greater than the sum of its parts.

The police service has accepted that partnerships are the most effective way forward, although to some extent they have done so as a result of a legal obligation placed on them by the Crime and Disorder Act 1998. This legislation, which fuels the argument that 'the police can no longer solve the drugs problem alone', seems to have been accepted without question, yet as Billingsley (1992) argues, partnerships will not succeed if the police continue to dominate all aspects of the work and other agencies allow them to do so. The drug problem seems to be a case in point where a multi-agency approach may not be always appropriate unless there is overall agreement about the aims and methods of the task in hand, and agreement about where responsibility lies for different aspects of the problem. For example social problems associated with drug abuse are best dealt with by the social services departments, where so-called collateral damage suffered by communities provides problems for local authorities (May *et al*, 1999: 1). On the other hand, acquisitive crime committed to support a drug habit is best dealt with by the police. Perhaps then it has to be acknowledged that although partnerships will and should exist there must be a division of labour between agencies, and it is unwise to believe the police should deal with all aspects of the problem. The police strategy ought to be one of intelligence-led policing, using sufficient resources to obtain and collate intelligence, and using that information to assist other agencies working alongside appropriate police units such as force drug squads and National Crime Squads. This would seem to be the way forward, amounting to an amended and modified approach to the partnership model.

Another difficulty with partnerships is that they tend to deal with the overt problem, whilst ignoring the driving force behind it. For example, if one assumes there is a problem of prostitution or burglary in a local community, it is likely the police will deal with this through the vice squad or burglary protection unit, in partnership of course with other specialist agencies concerned with prostitution or burglary. Yet the prostitution or burglary may be driven by a drug supply system which goes unrecognised or misunderstood, so that by dealing with the offenders according to their offences the source of the criminality goes unnoticed.

Partnerships seem not to be able to deal with these underlying structures. The reasons for this are sometimes unclear, but as far as the police are concerned they often relate to other demands, such as meeting targets set by performance indicators. Performance indicators are usually about the number of arrests, the extent of drug seizures, etc., rather than about the manner in which the police disrupt local drug markets or provide preventative measures to reduce demand. Worse than that, handlers are not always drug squad officers, giving rise to the view that information about drugs will not be taken up, the handler being concerned only about the offences which interest them (Billingsley, 2000).

Government policy statements on research, which seem to give a low priority to informers, do not always help the police. In a recent Home Office Paper entitled *'Policing drug hot spots'* (Home Office, PRG Paper 109) Jessica Jackson suggests that drug dealing can be expected to be at a higher level when there is a lack of surveillance, weak management, the presence of potential customers and the facilities for buying and using drugs (Jackson, 1999). All true; but there was no mention of informers in those 'hot spots'. The chances are there will be numerous participating informers in every drug market affecting the types of drugs sold, the structures of supply, and the numbers of arrests. It is odd that such a key variable should be ignored.

An important initiative which we think points to a way ahead relates to the use of dedicated handling units whose sole objective is to obtain relevant and meaningful intelligence by what are called 'tasking' informers. Dedicated units can take on the role of specialist drug squads and other specialisms such as burglary units; this in effect reduces the handler's discretion and restricts the way information can be selectively processed according to the interests of the handler – the so-called selectivity problem (Billingsley, 2000). Productivity in terms of arrests arising from dedicated units seems to have increased, as has the nature and extent of intelligence. Such an initiative, however, is not without its critics. Smaller forces, for example, complain that dedicated units are easily and quickly disbanded when it becomes necessary to staff a major investigation, and other critics suggest valuable intelligence is wasted because of an inefficient use of resources. Even so, dedicated handling units provide many advantages, not the least that the handlers will be carefully selected, thus avoiding some of the more glaring problems associated with inexperienced officers handling drug informers. These handlers can give a clear and more consistent picture of the problem, as well as building up experience of different kinds of methods. They are not the only solution by any means but they are an important one.

If informers are to be used successfully they must be 'tasked'. Drug users inevitably commit property crimes to sustain their habit and lifestyle. To be effective the informer must mix with a range of offenders, yet provide information as a 'tasked' operator; that is, to say informers can no longer be allowed to provide information on one type of crime, or on the crimes about which they want to inform. The informer must produce information on the crimes selected by the police; this is the essential feature of 'tasking'.

Drug abuse and its associated criminality continue to be a major problem, requiring all police forces to give it priority in their strategic plans. It is important that performance indicators, which after all are methods of determining success in meeting objectives, include the use of informers. These indicators should, *inter alia* determine the extent of use, the quality of information provided, the resulting action taken, and the crime patterns occurring as a result of the information received. Were this to be so it would provide another way in which the effectiveness of informers could be determined (in this respect it is interesting that a large proportion of offences relating to prostitution, begging and similar offences are drug driven yet the police apparently have no performance indicators to assess this).

It is neither possible nor desirable to ignore informers, and they are an important part of police practice. Controlling them effectively and ensuring that they work according to police requirements will require much greater attention than has been given to this hitherto. It will require an understanding of what informers can offer, and an equal understanding of the dangers they present, whether to the police, themselves or others.

However, set against this is the recent emphasis by senior police officers on non-enforcement rather than investigation. For example, the police have recently commissioned a new task force to advance crime reduction programmes which will inevitably concentrate on partnerships rather than investigatory skills, placing less emphasis on the use of informers and other forms of covert policing. There is no doubt crime reduction is important, as is drug education and harm reduction, but such strategies can only be part of the solution. Consideration still needs to be given to developing investigatory skills, and unless greater emphasis is placed on increasing training for handlers, including being aware of the dangers of informers, and considering their impact on the drug problem, policing will be undermined.

## Some concluding comments

Other chapters in this volume deal with some of the ethical issues surrounding the use of informers; here we want to touch on two of these as they affect the policing of drug markets. The first centres on juveniles. The peak age of crime stubbornly remains in the 15–18 age group, which is also the age at which most drug taking begins. Breaking into that world requires informers, some of whom must be of the same age. The ethical problems surrounding this are immense especially when payment for information, sometimes information about the juvenile's parents and family, is used to buy drugs.

The new codes of practice for informers advise that juveniles should only be used in exceptional circumstances, but this is hardly realistic. Information about juveniles is most likely to come from other juveniles. The Metropolitan Police Informant Working Group (1998) recommended that financial inducement or other material gifts should not be offered as a trigger for information or assistance (but could presumably be offered later), and that this should be fully explained to the child and their parents or guardians (p.9). Again, this is not satisfactory: it takes no account of those cases where the child informs on his or her family, nor where the information is of such a nature that it is likely to lead to the arrest of a serious criminal. Some police forces prohibit the use of juvenile informers, and whilst they may be commended for their moral stance, others will continue to use them. The only solution to the problem is to keep under close review and amend as appropriate the codes of practice and produce guidelines that are morally acceptable. They must take account of the age of the juvenile, the nature of the information and the likely use of any payment.

The second issue relates to the use of participating informers, especially those who are drug users. The question we want to ask is this: how can any police force take any serious part in multi-agency rehabilitation when its drug informers, who are often addicts, are being paid for their information, and it is likely that these rewards will be used to buy drugs? Or as Donnelly said in 1971, albeit in a different context, 'The spectacle of the [police] secretly mated with the underworld and using underworld characters to gain its ends is not an ennobling one.' (Donnelly, 1971). Moreover, participating informers are tasked with conducting intelligence, which requires them to associate with drug users. What chance do they stand of being rehabilitated?

This question strikes at the heart of all debates about informers, and is about ends justifying means. Is the use of the informer, distasteful though it may be, justified by the end results? The courts certainly think so, for they are prepared to offer reductions in the sentence for information received (see the Introduction, pp. 8–9). We think so too, although we recognise the force of the Kantian argument which says there is never a justification to use human beings as a means to some greater end. Sadly, the world is for us rather more complicated, but we think the Kantian position should be held out as a beacon to warn against the dangers of forgetting that informers are about betrayal, albeit betraying others who break the law.

The police, who police by the consent of the public, must give due regard to those who view with alarm the way informers appear to be granted some form of immunity, or continue to participate in crime (other equally important matters such as the protection of the informer's identity are dealt with elsewhere in this volume). At present there is no adequate alternative to the use of informers, but there is a point to be made about the way they are handled and controlled. Never has there been a better time for the police to put this particular aspect of their practice in order, including allowing greater public scrutiny of their activities. The police need to be ever more accountable if the use of informers is to be maintained as a legitimate investigative tool.

# References

Bean, P.T. (1992) 'Cocaine and crack in Nottingham. A follow up study'. Unpublished report to the Home Office.

Billingsley, R. (1992) 'The partnership approach to crime reduction'. Unpublished M.A. dissertation, University of Exeter.

Billingsley, R. (2000) 'An examination of the relationship between informers and handlers in the police service in England and Wales'. Unpublished Ph.D. thesis, University of Loughborough.

*Columbia Law School News* (1996) 'Informers in Federal narcotics prosecutions', *Columbia Journal of Law and Social Problems*, Vol. 2 (June): 47-54.

Donnelly, R.C. (1971) 'The judicial control of informants'. *Yale Law Journal*. Vol. 60: 1091-1131.

Dorn, N., Murji, K. and South, N. (1992) *Traffickers: drug markets and law enforcement*, London: Routledge.

Dunnighan, C. (1992) 'Reliable sources'. *Police Review*, 14 August: 1496-1497.

Grieve, J. (1992) 'The police contribution to drugs education: a role for the 1990s', in Evans, R. and O'Connor, L. (eds) *Drug Abuse and Misuse: Developing educational strategies in partnership*. Fulton: 53-64.

Goldstein, J. (1960) 'Police discretion not to invoke the criminal process in the administration of justice'. *Yale Law Journal*. Vol 69.

Home Office (1991) *Safer Communities: The local delivery of crime prevention through the partnership approach* (August).

Home Office (1969) *Informants who take part in crime.* Home Office Circular 97/1969 (12 May).

Jackson, J. (1999) *Policing drug hot spots.* Police Research Group, Home Office Paper, 109.

Khan, A.N. and Gillance K. (1976), 'Agent Provocateur', *Police Review,* 30 April: 536–538.

May, T., Edmunds, M. and Hough, M. (1999) *Street Business: The links between sex and drug markets.* Policing and Reducing Crime: Police Research Series, Paper 118 (Home Office).

Maynard, W. (1994) *Witness Intimidation. Strategies for prevention.* Police Research Group, Home Office, Paper 55.

Metropolitan Police Informant Working Group (1998) *Informing the Community. Developing Informant Risk Assessment to reflect community concerns.* Metropolitan Police/Police Complaints Authority (July).

Skolnick, J. (1967) *Justice without Trial.* New York: Wiley.

*Times* Law Reports: *Regina v Rankine* before Lord Chief Justice Lord Lane, 4 March 1986; *R. v Anthony Garner*; *R. v Preston and McAlery*, and *R. v Afzel*, 14 October 1989.

# 2  Informers and corruption

## Roy Clark

## Introduction

The dangers involved in recruiting and running informers are well recognised by law enforcement and similar agencies throughout the world. Within the UK police, informers are subject to continuous oversight and ever tightening regulations for by definition, and to be effective, police informers are closely connected to the criminal underworld and in most cases have engaged, or will engage, in crime themselves.

Considerable effort is made to ensure the law, the rules and the ethics of informer use are not transgressed (see other chapters in this volume). The fact that so much is achieved by informers in terms of arrests, recovered property, saving life and the prevention of crime, is in itself a testament to the high levels of use by police, and the approval given by the judicial system. The value of informers at a time when policing is increasingly intelligence-led cannot be doubted. The risk of allowing police officers to come into regular contact with criminals under controlled conditions is therefore justified. On almost every occasion the contacts, and resulting police actions, are conducted according to high ethical standards. There are, however, rare occasions when standards fall, supervision fails and people become vulnerable to temptation. Under such circumstances the dangers of informers and police officers becoming corrupt are high. It is also clear that some, already corrupt, seek to use the informer handling system as a cover for their activities.

The aim of this chapter is to explore informer-related corruption. It is written from the position of an operational police officer with data taken from recent events. Reference is made to specific cases, some of which have been disguised for obvious reasons. It draws on information and intelligence resulting from a study of police corruption undertaken by the Metropolitan Police over the last few years.

## Donald and Cressey – a classic case study

One of the most spectacular examples of informer-related corruption came to public notice in September 1993. Its origins can, however, be traced to the previous year when on the 1 September 1992 two prominent criminals, Kevin Cressey and David Fraser, were arrested in possession of 55 kilos of cannabis and a loaded firearm on the streets of south London. The arresting officers were from the Regional Crime Squad and amongst their number was Detective Constable John Donald, a long-serving and experienced member of the Metropolitan Police. In the hours immediately after his arrest Cressey, presumably convinced that the evidence against him was compelling, sought a way out of his predicament; he set about corrupting a police officer. His success in obtaining the corrupt services of Donald would become the subject of exposure on national television and a long and complex Old Bailey trial which ended with both men being sent to prison. Donald was sentenced to eleven years' imprisonment and Cressey to seven.

The case also brought together another small part of an intelligence picture of corruption being secretly built at Scotland Yard at the time. In particular, it became another graphic example of the role informers had in a small but pernicious area of criminal activity which in turn led to the creation of the Metropolitan Police anti-corruption squad and a new campaign against corruption.

Whilst being detained at the police station, Cressey gave subtle hints that he had valuable information and was willing to become an informer. Over the course of several hours in police custody a number of officers attempted to cultivate him as an informer but without success. Clearly he did not see in those officers the signs of dishonesty which he was looking for and so rejected their approach. Eventually John Donald entered the cell and it is evident the two recognised in each other the possibility that the other could be exploited for mutual gain. Their relationship was almost certainly corrupt from the very beginning, but to allow it to flourish Cressey had to be registered as an informer. Registration would enable the two men, at opposite ends of the criminal justice spectrum, to engage in forms of corruption whilst under the cover of legitimacy and under the noses and supervision of police managers. Police officer and criminal cannot have regular and legitimate contact in any other way without attracting attention.

After being charged with serious criminal offences Cressey was bailed but contact with Donald was maintained under the guise of informer and informer handler. The first clear but major act of corruption centred upon Cressey's determination to avoid being convicted for drug dealing and receiving which would result in a long sentence of imprisonment. They agreed that for the sum of £40,000 Donald would remove and destroy the original observation log detailing the events leading to the arrests. This would almost certainly cause any case brought against Cressey to fail in a spectacular fashion, and would probably lead to allegations of incompetence or even of perjury against other honest officers. As a down payment Cressey handed Donald £18,000 in cash. An attempt was made to steal the observation logs but it was thwarted by an honest officer.

It is interesting that during the relationship, or perhaps even at the beginning, the roles of Cressey and Donald became reversed. That is to say, the criminal became the informer handler and the police officer became the informer. For example, Donald provided Cressey with highly secret intelligence concerning police target operations against major criminals by accessing intelligence computer systems. He received payment for his information, using his ability to conduct apparently legitimate meetings with his 'informer' to conduct his criminal business. This so-called role reversal will be a major theme of this chapter with various examples given as to how it operates.

Whilst the information provided by Donald was obviously advantageous to Cressey, and it is probable that he made money by passing it on to others, nonetheless he was almost certainly facing imprisonment for his crimes. In an attempt to discredit Donald and bring down the case against him Cressey approached a television company giving his side of the story. Over several weeks Donald was filmed meeting Cressey and their conversations were taped. The programme was screened on 27 September 1993. Subsequently both men were arrested and eventually convicted. Cressey, attempting to undermine the prosecution by revealing the extent of corruption involved, had overlooked the fact that both giver and taker of a bribe are equally guilty. A clear pattern of corruption had been established long before he decided to expose Donald.

## The anti-corruption initiative at Scotland Yard

At the same time that Donald and Cressey were committing their crimes there was growing recognition at Scotland Yard that major criminals were engaged in corruption with a few, but importantly placed police officers. They too were acting under the cover of the informer/handler relationship. Two senior detectives within the criminal intelligence branch (SO11) analysed the information, albeit in an unconventional manner, and noticed that a small number of criminals received immunity from police attention and a degree of protection from arrest. Moreover, the criminals seemed to be confident that even if arrested they could buy their way out of trouble, and could rely on a small group of corrupt police officers for information, advice and a range of other criminal services. The analysis continued throughout 1992 and into 1993 under a cloak of secrecy and led later to a report submitted to the Commissioner, Sir Paul Condon. This report alerted him to the problem of police corruption. It suggested that a secret intelligence gathering operation should be established to produce a greater understanding of the nature, methods and personalities of corruption.

Approval and funding was obtained, and so began what is arguably one of the most adventurous policing operations of recent times. Over the course of the next two years a secret squad of police officers gathered intelligence which enabled a more sophisticated understanding of the corrupt relationships between criminals and a few police officers to be achieved. Whilst the numbers involved were not large it became clear that the potential damage to the reputation of the police service and the criminal justice system was immense.

## The reversal of informant and handler roles

What became clear from this study was the degree to which informers were an important element in corruption. Whilst the use of the informer handling system as a cover for criminal activity was apparent, and indeed the possibility of such abuse of a vital policing tool had long been recognised, a new and more sinister problem became visible. There was evidence that, as with Cressey and Donald, there was a complete reversal of the roles of the police officer and the informer. The informer with a criminal record or background became the recipient of police intelligence, whilst the police officer became the informer. Moreover, whilst the criminals would not recognise it in such precise terms, it became clear that this reversal process led to the criminals adopting many of the elements of police practices which relate to the recruitment and use of police officer informers. It was found that the criminals developed their own policy or set of standards which closely mirrored the accepted law enforcement practices. These include the active recruitment of informers, protection from exposure, the use of pseudonyms, an acknowledgement that intelligence is to be shared, the tasking of informers, the provision of more than one handler, and reward in cash commensurate with the value of intelligence provided. It was as a result of this breakthrough that significant tactical advantage was given to the overt phase of the Metropolitan Police anti-corruption campaign that was to follow.

All police officers are taught the value of intelligence and the merit of recruiting informers. It is accepted good practice for every arrested person to be considered as a potential source of information. Experienced officers develop a sixth sense as to whether a prisoner is capable of being recruited and the sort of information he or she may give. It is at the time of arrest and processing that police officer and prisoner legitimately spend considerable periods of time in each other's company. Frequently the first step is taken by the prisoner who, realising the strength of evidence against them and facing the inevitability of conviction and knowing too that courts take such factors into account, seeks to assist the police by offering details of the criminal activities of others.

Whilst the case of Cressey and Donald is one example of criminals recognising that the tables can be turned there have been others, the most graphic of which involves a criminal who, for reasons of sensitivity, will simply be called 'Able'. He is an older man and a lifetime criminal who specialises in offences of so called high-value burglary. Following a lengthy surveillance operation he and others were arrested in London in 1997. Whilst 'Able' was being questioned and subsequently charged he made a number of cryptic remarks to the two officers dealing with him. There was nothing very obvious in what he said but the detectives gained the clear impression that they were being sounded out with corruption in mind. They were, like over 99 per cent of their colleagues, good and honest people and voiced their suspicions to officers from the Metropolitan Police anti-corruption squad. After careful assessment of the law and ethics involved the detectives were given authority to draw out 'Able' and explore his suggestions. Strict conditions and terms of reference were required including the need to record all conversations, alongside directions that the officers should never take the lead or force the situation. Any corrupt suggestion or hint of the same had to come from 'Able'. The prisoner, faced with two apparently compliant detectives, quickly moved forward with his plan and very soon was making clear and specific suggestions as to how the officers could help him and how they could benefit financially. He even insisted that he be registered as the officer's informer as this gave both parties an element of protection and presented opportunities for abusing the reward system for their mutual benefit.

Over several months the relationship between 'Able' and his police handlers developed but only under conditions that ensured that good quality evidence was being obtained. During these conversations 'Able' made the startling revelation that throughout a criminal career of over thirty years he had always regarded any period of detention or arrest as an ideal opportunity to try to corrupt police officers. As a result of this operation 'Able' and a number of his criminal associates were convicted and imprisoned for offences relating to corruption. Whilst enquiries into his long criminal career continue in so far as it relates to other possible offences of police corruption, it is clear that in the vast majority of instances his approaches would have been rebuffed. Officers would have dealt with it either by ignoring it or warning 'Able' that in making corrupt suggestions he and others like him were in danger of committing a criminal offence. However, whilst such a response is entirely appropriate and usually given at times when officers are busy dealing with other offences, it leaves the corrupter free to corrupt elsewhere. Moreover it serves to conceal the danger. It is also possible that police officers have not dealt with these suggestions more positively because there has been a lack of clear guidance on corruption, and there has not been a department within the police force with a responsibility for providing guidance or undertaking covert operations against corrupters. With the new insights being gained into corruption most police forces are introducing professional standards units which will adopt a pro-active strategy and fill the void.

A second police policy relating to the use of informers which has been taken over by criminals is the notion that they should be protected from identification. One device used by police to ensure that an identity is protected is to use pseudonyms, where the real identity of the informer is known only to a very few and then under strict control conditions. For example, the secret phase of the anti-corruption operation within the Metropolitan Police made use of intelligence-gathering techniques and, again, produced fascinating evidence of the reversal of law enforcement standards. It became clear that any criminal who had successfully corrupted an officer would exercise great care not to give information that would give a clue as to his identity. There would never be a reference to the officer's place or type of work, personal habits or life style. If the criminal used a name it was almost always a pseudonym. One such pseudonym served to illustrate that there is rarely affection by the criminal towards the corrupt officer and that police officer informers are held in contempt by their new handlers. This came as a shock to one corrupt officer who, during questioning, was told that he was known as 'Babe – The Talking Pig' after the film of the same name. Understandably he was somewhat disturbed by what he saw as disloyalty.

Other lengths to which criminals will go to prevent their valuable police sources being discovered include complicated systems for making contact, involving systems of calls from telephone kiosks (as shown in the television programme exposing Donald), and the exercise of great care should personal meetings become necessary, whether to exchange cash or provide sensitive material. Surveillance operations to detect and provide evidence of corrupt contacts have been undertaken by experienced police officers which have involved watching some of the most expert criminals in the country, but even they have been stretched to the limit of their skills.

Paradoxically the criminal stresses the need for caution whereas the corrupt officer often seems more relaxed about contacts and meetings. Why should this be so? It is suggested this can be explained in one of two ways. Firstly, corrupt police officers are over confident; they are aware of actions against them based on their knowledge of police intelligence or of evidence-gathering techniques, and above all are aware that, until recently, few police forces had the ability to respond to corrupt practices. Or, secondly, the corrupter places significant value on the relationship and recognises that his continued liberty, or that of his associates, depends upon it. So for example, after the public exposure of Donald, intelligence reports indicated that many prominent criminals were amazed that one of their number could destroy what was for them a valuable source of information and protection. One criminal reported that he was considering violence against Cressey as Cressey's actions would, he thought, make the recruitment of police officer informers more difficult. Again there is an interesting parallel here where the use of formal or informal discipline within the police service is used for any officer who endangers the integrity of the informer handling system for want of care.

It has long been an important part of police philosophy that officers must realise informers are not the personal property of the handler but are a resource to be used for the benefit of law enforcement as a whole. There is evidence from a number of corruption enquiries that criminals also share such a belief so far as police officer informers are concerned. One highly detailed intelligence report revealed that an active criminal based in the east of London recognised the value of such an asset and went to some lengths to advertise the services available amongst his underworld associates, whilst taking great care not to reveal the identity of the officer. This information provided rich pickings for the anti-corruption detectives. Similar evidence was obtained against Donald who was filmed and presented to television viewers, providing Cressey with highly secret information about police operations against a number of his associates. Various sums of money were paid for Donald's services with Cressey taking the responsibilities of a handler for and on behalf of the criminal underworld as a whole. Even so, it is likely that there was a difference between the price paid for this information and the amount handed to Donald; the criminal handler would have taken his cut.

An early corruption investigation produced quality intelligence and some evidence of what is called the tasking of a corrupted police source aimed at providing information for a person under surveillance. The criminal suspected he may have been the subject of surveillance but he did not know which squad was watching him or how much they knew. Reports revealed that he first made enquiries to establish if any of his associates knew of a corrupt officer who could help him. Once he established that there was such an officer he told him what he wanted and negotiated a price. Again, this is another example of a reversal of one of the fundamental and important elements of the law enforcement informant handling system – informers are tasked with specific operational requirements; in this case so were the corrupt police officers

Criminals will seek to corrupt anyone who can offer information they can turn to their own advantage. Whilst this chapter has been written mainly from a police perspective it would be wrong to consider that the police service is the only agency within the wider criminal justice system vulnerable to corruption or penetration by criminals. In March 2000 Mark

Herbert, a Crown Prosecution Service official with access to sensitive computer systems data, was sentenced to six years' imprisonment at the Old Bailey. He was convicted of conspiring to provide what the sentencing Judge called a 'notorious and feared' London-based criminal family with the identities of 33 police informers. The case against Herbert was that he obtained information for a criminal gang who knew of his place of employment and the type of intelligence at his disposal. His reward was just £1,000, although the court heard he hoped to receive a great deal more.

At the time Herbert was being sentenced another trial at the Old Bailey involved other allegations of corruption. Kailesh Sawnhey, an official within HM Customs and Excise office at Heathrow, pleaded guilty to offences relating to corruption. He admitted passing secrets to an organised criminal gang engaged in drug dealing and smuggling, and passing on details of operations against them on computer systems. Again the money received was considerable.

Whilst criminals cherish and protect their police sources and go to considerable lengths to conceal their true identities, there is evidence that they also mirror police practice by introducing a co-handler or second person to manage contact with a corrupted officer. One of the reasons for dual handling by the police is that, coupled with high levels of control and other security measures, dual handling goes some way to preserve the integrity of the relationship. It also ensures that one of the handlers will be available at all times. Ethics and quality assurance do not, of course, have any part to play in the thinking of criminals, but they are able nonetheless to recognise the advantages of having more than one person who can make contact with a corrupt police officer. This was particularly so in the case of a criminal who will be known as 'Baker'. He found that it was important to have a second person to approach should he be arrested and remanded in custody. To this end he congratulated himself on having the foresight to introduce his police source to a second criminal associate, having been conscious that such a difficulty might arise if he were to find himself detained and unable to conduct business with the corrupt officer when his need was greatest.

Giving rewards for the supply of information is perhaps the most obvious way in which the formal police informant handling system is mirrored by the criminal underworld. Elsewhere in this chapter there has been reference to the types of sum available: Donald was seen on national television and heard to discuss 'thirty and ten large' (£30,000 and £10,000) for the destruction of one sheet of paper vital to a prosecution; Herbert received only £1,000 but expected to be paid much more for information about police informants. Clearly the corrupted officers have a view about the value of their services, with the corrupters having an understanding that information aimed at protecting their liberty is of great value. Such sums are easily found by criminals, particularly by those involved in the drugs trade where the risks are high but the profit massive. The payment of large rewards is seen simply as an operational overhead or as an investment to secure the prolonged viability of their business. The money is hardly missed and soon replaced.

This realisation that there has been an almost complete reversal of the law enforcement informant handling system should not come as a surprise. After all, the concept of a double agent is not new and double agents have presented both opportunities and threats to intelligence agencies throughout the world. Running an agent or handling an informer operate on the same common sense basis. Criminals are generally resourceful people possessed of considerable levels of common sense, honed by high degrees of cunning and determination. It makes sense that they should recruit informers from within the organisation whose task it is to bring them down. It makes sense, too, that they should seek to protect their sources and give them pseudonyms, that they should share intelligence, direct informers to their specific needs and provide co-handlers for the same purpose. It makes abundant sense that they should invest part of their considerable profits in business continuity. Now that those facts have been recognised the operational advantage presented to the police service becomes considerable.

## Informants and police as partners in crime

In December 1997 Kevin Garner, a recently retired police officer, a serving police officer named McGuinness and a third man were filmed by anti-corruption squad detectives breaking into a flat in the Limehouse district of London. They had in their possession what appeared to be a search warrant and they were looking for drugs. Clearly they were acting on information. The presence of an ex-officer, the lack of a genuine search warrant and the absence of prior authority from a supervising officer indicated that from the very beginning this was a criminal enterprise. Having entered they found over 80 kilograms of cannabis which they removed. A few days later the three were arrested and charged with offences of aggravated burglary and drug dealing.

Faced with such overwhelming evidence, and having been shown the police video of their crime, Garner and McGuinness confessed and admitted over twenty other offences of major corruption. They subsequently pleaded guilty at the Old Bailey. These offences included drug possession, thefts of large sums of cash and conspiracy to rob. It should be recorded that the third man denied involvement and was acquitted. The confessions of a serving and a retired police officer added significantly to a picture that was then building up about crimes conducted by police officers, some of which involved informers as partners. For legal reasons it is not yet possible to give further detail of the offences admitted, but the main facts of the case are set out for they illustrate the levels of criminality involved, and highlight further the dangers of informers to law enforcement agencies.

Further evidence of an alliance of informers and police officer involves the case of Evelyna Fleckney, a registered police informer, who was sentenced to 15 years' imprisonment in 1998 after being convicted of drug dealing offences. The evidence was that she had been a significant middle-level dealer in drugs throughout south London for several years, and that she controlled a number of men who helped in her criminal trade. During her trial she revealed that she was an informer and stated that she was acting under the instructions of her handler, an officer who, for legal reasons, will be called 'Charlie'. Police saw the relationship between Fleckney and 'Charlie' as highly corrupt and sexual. It was agreed by the prosecution that the police officer would be called and was to be questioned by the defence. From the witness box the officer denied he had given authority to his informer to deal in drugs or that he and Fleckney were having an affair. Shortly after she had begun her prison sentence Fleckney was visited by anti-corruption squad officers. She confessed that she and 'Charlie' had had a corrupt relationship for some years and gave details that would confirm that they were indeed lovers. She had used her knowledge of London drug dealers to provide her handler with considerable quantities of drugs. The officer 'Charlie' conducted the searches and seized the drugs, only a proportion of which was used to support prosecutions. The rest was handed to her by 'Charlie' for her to sell for their mutual financial benefit

## Informants and corruption outside the criminal justice system

We live in what has been called the information age and in a time when a mass of detail is placed in computer systems for the use of all. Within the United Kingdom we are about to have freedom of information legislation which rightly requires public organisations to be open and accountable. There will, however, always be legitimate secrets both in the public and private sectors. Leakage of information about the financial intentions of Government, or business or insider information of many kinds is often worth a fortune and, under some circumstances, could amount to corruption. Within the business sector it could also lead to an investigation by the Serious Fraud Office or by one of several regulatory bodies or even to civil action. There has been at least one incident in recent years where one company recruited an informer from within another at the time of a hostile take-over bid. The existence of the informer became known and was made the subject of a sophisticated private investigation and surveillance operation which produced photographic and other evidence of corruption. The predator company, faced with public and humiliating disclosure, retreated at considerable cost in terms of reputation and money. How many similar cases there are in what is a very closed world is a matter of conjecture, but it is probable that informers and corruption are as much a problem outside the criminal justice systems as they are within it.

## Informants as a response to corruption

Whilst much of this chapter has been focused on the negative nature of a few informer and handler relationships it is necessary to stress that such cases are few and, with increased realisation of the dangers, now more readily capable of detection. Moreover it is encouraging that informers themselves have had a positive part to play in many of the corruption cases being placed before the courts. They also have a significant role in the anti-corruption strategies now being adopted by UK law enforcement. Few corrupt relationships involving a criminal and a police officer exist in secrecy or without somebody being aware of the possibility of unlawful behaviour. Pseudonyms may mask the identity of a corrupt officer but the possibility of the existence of such a person is frequently all that is required for an investigation to commence and for arrests to follow. Whilst it was the actions of 'Charlie' himself that led to his relationship with Fleckney coming to the fore, the subsequent investigation revealed that many of her criminal associates were aware of her involvement with a corrupt police officer who was partner and protector. Indeed she used the relationship as a threat to others if they sought to challenge her in their drug dealing hierarchy. Clearly whilst she considered this gave her increased authority it also added significantly to her vulnerability.

Informants have been an important source of information to the Metropolitan Police in secret intelligence gathering operations which led to the present anti-corruption campaign. They have introduced several lines of enquiry and added significantly to others. Whilst it is clear that much of the criminal underworld values a corrupt source of information the basic truth is that there is no such thing as honour amongst thieves. Rivalry, jealousy and the settling of old scores create high levels of instability within criminal circles and ensure a constant stream of information to the police. Informers are also a vital component of any strategic response to corruption.

## Conclusion

Informers and their links with treachery and corruption are not a new phenomenon. The ethics relating to the use of informers has been a subject of comment and debate throughout time. There remain conflicting messages and we consider concepts of freedom of information and the need for secrecy in a society in which transparency is a virtue. From Judas to Philby questions about informers, what they do and why they do it, remain fascinating to us. However, the law has recognised that informers have an important part to play in ensuring public safety and has issued guidance on their use which, if contravened, may render a prosecution void and those involved subject to censure or even criminal investigation. Police welcome this guidance because it ensures that there is regulation and direction given to officers in the discharge of their responsibilities, which retain the liberty of the citizen at its core.

The examples used in this chapter might create an impression that corruption in and around the use of informers is rampant and out of control. It is not. Almost all contacts between police officers and informers, and there are thousands of such contacts each week, are conducted according to the highest possible ethical standards and are the subject of considerable levels of supervision and oversight. The public benefit as a consequence is that the police are given information on the most serious crimes. The anti-corruption initiatives of the Metropolitan Police are being followed by law enforcement agencies throughout the country. In April 2000 the Association of Chief Police Officers unveiled its own anti-corruption strategy and handed to Chief Constables advice on how to assess the vulnerability of their forces to corruption with particular emphasis on the dangers and risks of informer use. There should be public confidence in the increasingly high standards of informer control and the criminal trials used as examples should serve to illustrate the police's determination to become as corruption free as humanly possible. The convictions of Donald, Cressey, Fleckney and others will certainly act as a deterrent to others, be they informer or police officer, who may become tempted.

There are three particular lessons to learn from the events of the past few years. The first is that corruption in all walks of life is inevitable, but the levels of inevitability are significantly increased when police officers, of necessity, interact with informers with criminal backgrounds. The second is that any form of unethical or criminal behaviour involving an informer or handler can be detected in spite of the permitted cover of secrecy and, significantly, successful prosecutions with long prison sentences do follow. The third, and probably most important lesson, is that the high-risk nature of the relationships between informers and their handlers should always be the subject of intrusive and intelligence-led supervision and surveillance. If the present very high standards are allowed to fall, if corruption by and with informers should increase or go unchecked, the courts will lose confidence in their use. The loss to policing and thereby the public will be massive and the benefit to organised and not so organised criminals vast.

# 3 The ethics of informer handling

## Tom Williamson and Peter Bagshaw

## Introduction

Most law enforcement officials accept that informers are the most cost-effective means of dealing with serious and organised crime. An important caveat however, is that the use of informers carries risks. Where the risk management of informers has fallen down it can usually be traced to a lack of integrity.

The recent history of law enforcement in England points to a systemic lack of integrity that is tantamount to institutionalised corruption. There is no shortage of evidence of unprincipled informer handling. Fortunately the police service has work in progress to put in place checks and balances to correct the situation, including protecting the organisation against employees who use informers corruptly, or are corrupted by them. This chapter will consider actual and perceived institutionalised corruption. It will then examine the ethical dilemmas that surround the police use of informers in an effort to assess whether such a practice can ever be ethically justified.

The story of police deviance has been recounted many times in both the popular press and academic literature and will no doubt continue to excite interest. Nearly twenty years have passed since surveys in London showed that a large proportion of the public believed that when questioning suspects the police use unnecessary force, fabricate evidence and take bribes (Smith, 1983; Williamson, 1990). Since then the Metropolitan Police have suffered further damage as a result of the publicity arising from cases involving the mismanagement of informers. Particularly embarrassing was the case of Eaton Green, a known criminal who was in the UK unlawfully and being sought in connection with serious offences in his own country, but was still used by the Metropolitan Police as an informer. During this time he also committed further serious, violent offences. The mismanagement of this particular informer led to an enquiry supervised by the Police Complaints Authority and conducted by Sir John Hoddinott, who at that time was Chief Constable of Hampshire.

His report was not published but it is believed that he found poor systems, ineffective leadership and a lack of accountability.

More recently there have been the unsubstantiated allegations made by Counsel for the parents of Stephen Lawrence, a black teenager who was murdered in a racially motivated attack. The investigation by the Metropolitan Police into his murder has been the subject of a public inquiry. Quite late on into the inquiry Stephen's father, Mr Lawrence said,

> I would say that both racism and corruption played a part in this
> investigation.... As to corruption I think that some police officers
> investigating my son's death were connected to the murderers in some way
> or other. We keep hearing all sorts of rumours...
>
> (MacPherson, 1999: 43)

Mr Mansfield, QC for Mr Lawrence, put the allegation to the inquiry in this way: 'We shall be asking the inquiry to draw such inferences – namely that there must have been collusion between members of the criminal fraternity and some police officers.'

The inquiry when considering these allegations applied the criminal standard of proof, that is to say it could only reach a conclusion if satisfied beyond all reasonable doubt that collusion or corruption was established. The inquiry concluded, 'It is right that we should say at once that no collusion or corruption is proved to have infected the investigation of Stephen Lawrence's murder. It would be wrong and unfair to conclude otherwise.'

It is important to note that this conclusion also covered the so-called 'Norris factor', which is said to have involved the 'pulling of punches' and the deliberate slowing down and 'fudging' of the investigation, so that the suspects, in particular David Norris, were protected and ineffectively pursued during the whole of the first investigation. Clifford Norris, the father of the suspect David Norris, was a criminal who was not arrested until the second investigation into the murder of Stephen Lawrence, although he was wanted on warrant. At the time of the inquiry he was in prison for offences involving drug dealing. It is clear from the line of questioning pursued by Counsel for the Lawrence family that the allegation of police corruption stemmed from their perception that the ineffective investigation into the murder of their son was due in part to the police protecting informers. It is a moot point whether the inquiry would have come to a different conclusion had they used the lower burden of proof, the balance of probabilities.

Concerns about corruption in the police are not new. According to Cox, Shirley and Short (1977: 9), as a result of what happened between 1969 and 1972, 'a score of London detectives went to gaol, hundreds more left the force in disgrace and the old CID hierarchy was savagely restructured. The myth of the London bobby was badly dented and a long-standing tradition of detective work was almost completely destroyed'. They called this 'The Fall of Scotland Yard'. Since then we have seen a regular pattern involving the revelation of unprincipled policing followed by reforms which have brought improvements. However, these have so far proved insufficient to prevent further examples of corruption, which continue to involve the relationship between detectives and active criminals who were being paid as informants. According to Mr Frank Williamson, one of Her Majesty's Inspectors of Constabulary appointed to examine corruption in the Metropolitan Police, only three sorts of detective existed in the Force. Those who were corrupt, those who knew others were corrupt but did nothing about it, and those who were too stupid to notice what was going on around them. This was because 'a small proportion of senior officers had grown up in a tradition of dishonesty' (Cox, Shirley and Short, 1977: 38).

Organisational changes were introduced and Sir Robert Mark, the Commissioner of Police for the Metropolis, felt able to write in his 1983 Annual Report,

> There is, of course, no way in which we can ensure that a police officer, any more than any other person, will do no wrong, but the number who do is diminishing. What we can do is to ensure that complaints of wrongdoing are dealt with impartially and thoroughly, and I think this Force can claim the most effective system for dealing with internal wrongdoing to be found in any organisation in the country.

Mark and his successors created a perception that the problem of corruption was being tackled rigorously. In 1985 the Metropolitan Police published *The Principles of Policing and Guidance for Professional Behaviour*, a book which was widely distributed but was not supported by any management effort to challenge and change the organisational culture. It was mere gloss. Public concern shifted from the venal behaviour of a minority of officers who had received bribes in exchange for favours given to suspects and began to focus instead on a more pervasive form of institutionalised corruption, the 'verballing' of suspects. This was a method used to fabricate confessions or damaging admissions. Where a suspect had confessed there was no way that honest officers could demonstrate that the confession had been voluntary. These concerns led to the Royal Commission on Criminal Procedure (1981) and legislative reforms of police processes brought about by the Police and Criminal Evidence Act (1984) and codes of practice which regulate the arrest, detention and questioning of suspects. As a result of the way the reforms were adopted by the police and strictly interpreted by the courts there was a feeling within the service that the problem of corruption and unethical policing practice had in reality been 'managed out'. The police were perceived to be growing in professionalism. Subsequent events have proved this to be uninformed and complacent. This complacency was first challenged in a prescient insight given in a speech delivered in 1992 by Sir John Woodcock, then Her Majesty's Chief Inspector of Constabulary. He argued,

> The work place values of the modern police service have not yet fully cut free of the past and the police service faces a massive task, if it is to hold, as the community now demands, integrity and respect for human rights, above all other considerations.

In drawing attention to what he called 'noble cause corruption' Sir John Woodcock argued that 'most of those who go wrong in this way are misguided rather than evil, and their actions are as a result of our collective failures as supervisors'. Alderson (1999: 68) reminds us:

> Police often see themselves as a thin line pitted against dark forces in society, which demand sacrifices on their own part. To corrupt oneself in the cause of convicting criminals is regarded as being justified at the expense of oneself. This frame of mind has given rise to the term 'noble cause corruption' which is a euphemism for perjury, which is a serious crime.

Woodcock did not believe in 'bad apples' – officers who are corrupt and commit criminal offences. Instead he considered the problem to be organisational deviance. 'It is not one of individual predisposition to wrongdoing but of structure, or what I have earlier called cultural failure.' He thought that any attempt by the Royal Commission on Criminal Justice (1992) to guarantee the integrity of police evidence would fail 'unless the police service itself changes its culture dramatically'. In his view the police were a nineteenth-century institution being dragged into the twenty-first century. The service needed to reinvent itself, 'with a style which draws its legitimacy from an understanding of current public needs and of the nature of the contract between police and a new generation of the public' (Woodcock, 1992).

For the next seven years this clarion call went unheeded as a 'new public management' agenda took over with its emphasis on 'effectiveness and efficiency'. The focus was on what the police do, rather than what the police are. Charman and Savage (1999) argue that this limits 'to the study of how well the police do what they do, rather than what they are there for'. Until recently there has been little effort, either by the service itself or by academia, to generate a philosophy of policing. In the absence of such a doctrine setting out the fundamental beliefs of what the police are for, the accountability of the police has been achieved through the introduction of a performance culture that has focussed on a raft of interim key performance indicators, such as crime clear-up rates. These indicators did not attempt to evaluate outcomes such as 'Is my community safer?' or 'Has crime been reduced?' That this situation should have arisen is perhaps not surprising; if there is no clarity about what the police are for, there will be little chance of identifying whether the huge resources being poured into policing are achieving the desired outcomes.

If Williamson (1973) and Woodcock (1992) were right and the police service was endemically corrupt the response to the introduction of a performance management regime would be to falsify the figures on which the police were being measured. In 1996 the Nottinghamshire Police faced such allegations following an internal inquiry. A television programme broadcast in March 1999 (Davis) provided examples of cases accepted as having been 'cleared up' when the police had made no inquiries to establish whether an offence had been committed in the first place, or whether there was evidence to support confessions. These confessions were usually obtained from officers visiting offenders serving terms of imprisonment, in order to 'clear up' their outstanding offences which had not been formally dealt with by a court. This was a practice encouraged by Her Majesty's Inspector of Constabulary in guidance circulated to Chief Constables in January 1987 and July 1996 (HMI, 1996).

One response of the Nottinghamshire Police was to create professional standards guidance. This was based on the following five principles: honesty, fairness, working together, accountability and communication. Like the Metropolitan Police before it, these professional standards were not supported by any management programme intended to challenge and change the organisational culture.

In 1998 Her Majesty's Inspector of Constabulary announced a thematic inspection into police integrity, which reported in June 1999. Once again it drew attention to a police culture characterised by ambiguous ethical values, where senior officers were criticised for accepting gratuities and free hospitality. Accepting free invitations to major sporting occasions, civic entertainment and even perceived lavish official facilities, is seen by junior staff as 'double standards'. A good practice guide gave 33 separate recommendations regarding the investigation and prosecution of offenders, of which 17 related to the recruitment and use of informers. This marks a significant point in the attempts by the police service to professionalise its management of informers. The future will show whether these attempts will continue to be undermined by the dubious ethical values of some individual officers, reflecting the continuation of institutionalised corruption within a police service which tolerates their standards in practice.

# The utilitarian case for informant handling

The following section of this chapter examines the ethical strengths and weaknesses of the use of informers from a philosophical point of view and questions whether informer handling can ever be conducted ethically. It considers the ethical dilemmas that arise from using informers; firstly by assuming that it is done with total compliance to existing rules and procedures, and then secondly, in its current flawed state. An informer is defined here as 'an individual... who is giving information about crime..., will typically have a criminal history, habits or associates, and will be giving the information freely whether or not in the expectation of a reward, financial or otherwise' (ACPO and HM Customs and Excise, 1999).

The use of informers as an intelligence source derives its strength from two main sources; firstly, from the general pursuit of intelligence as part of the move away from 'reactive' and toward 'proactive' policing (Cooper and Murphy, 1997: 1); and secondly, from its long tradition and history in social control and law enforcement (Dunnighan and Norris, 1998: 21).

Rising crime rates, exhortation from the Home Office, Her Majesty's Inspector of Constabulary and the Audit Commission, greater financial accountability throughout the criminal justice system and the growth of a new 'managerialism' (Raine and Wilson, 1995) have caused a swing towards so called 'intelligence-led' or proactive policing. Some argue that these pressures, combined with the decline of traditional 'confessional' and forensic evidence, have dictated an increased use of intelligence-based tactics like surveillance, undercover operations and informers to facilitate 'sting-type' convictions (Phillips, 1999). Far from representing a new development, 'the use of informants as a source of criminal intelligence is a practice as old as policing itself' (Cooper and Murphy, 1997: 1). Others trace it back to before formal policing began (Dunnighan and Norris, 1998: 21).

Advocates claim proactive policing is more efficient than reactive policing and that by freeing up resources it creates a virtuous circle that will ultimately reduce the need for reactive policing (Phillips, 1999). The relative expense of surveillance and undercover operations make the increased use of informers very attractive in these times of 'best value' and 'efficiency plans' (Local Government Act 1999 and Best Value Guidance and the Local Government [Best Value] Performance Plans and Reviews Order 1999).

Influential research carried out suggests that the costs per detection are unbeatable (Audit Commission, 1993) although it was later conceded that it had to form part of a co-ordinated 'crime strategy' for maximum benefit (Audit Commission, 1996). Figures from Merseyside from April 1994 to February 1995 show that by paying informers £55k they recovered £0.8m in stolen property, £0.75m in drugs, 13 firearms, achieved 450 arrests and one murder conviction (Cooper and Murphy, 1997: 3). Those who see the battle against crime as a war believe 'An army without spies is like a man with no ears or eyes' (Clavell, 1981: 95). Recognising these strengths, can our informer system be justified ethically?

A perfect system would never mislead the informer, the public or the justice system. However, all proactive techniques like the use of informers, surveillance and undercover operations rely on deceiving the target (Kleinig, 1996) and so can only be morally justified by rationalisation. This usually takes the so called 'fourfold route to justification' which can be summarised briefly as follows:

- deception is essential to achieve this particular task;

- the achievement of this task is essential to carry out the role;

- the role is essential to the effectiveness of the service;

- the service is necessary and justified and therefore the deception is necessary and justified (Bowling, 1999).

There is then a 'truth *versus* loyalty' dilemma if we accept that honesty is a moral imperative for the police *per se* and that therefore we should not deceive anyone at all, including targeted suspects. The good of the individual (be it the informer put in danger or the target caught out by deception) *versus* the good of the community protected from potential future harm presents an obvious dilemma.

The short-term advantage of catching an offender against a potential long-term disadvantage would seem unproblematic but some argue that an historical perspective has shown that serious problems can arise in an informer-based society. These problems stem from a decline in public support if informers are perceived to become too invasively used (Parker, 1999), or gain too much advantage from what is largely perceived as a distasteful activity (Cooper and Murphy, 1997). Here too, then, a dilemma exists. The justice-*versus*-mercy paradigm may cause a dilemma for some, but due to the essential role of the police this is significantly weakened by the duty to uphold the law. However, the use of individual discretion and the guiding principle of 'fairness' create clear potential dilemmas for individual officers.

Informer usage then arguably fits all four paradigms and since only one fit is necessary, this issue clearly exhibits potential ethical dilemmas. This established, can Kidder's 'resolution principles' (Kidder, 1992) help to justify informer usage? Stated simply, Kidder's three principles are

- 'Ends-based' (utilitarianism – the greatest good for the greatest number);

- 'Rules-based' (Kantian – follow your highest sense of principle), and

- 'Care-based' (do what you would want others to do to you?).

## Ends-based thinking

Ends-based thinking could justify a perfectly operated informant system. The need to tackle high crime rates and to spend public money responsibly would be sufficient cause to justify a degree of deception in our dealings, particularly where those deceived can be regarded as having forfeited their right to fair treatment by indulging in crime (Cooper and Murphy, 1997). This argument is strengthened further where the crimes in question are 'consensual transactions' such as drug dealing or vice where informer usage is often the only effective way of tackling them due to the lack of a traditional 'victim' or 'aggrieved' (Dunnighan and Norris, 1996a; also Phillips, 1999).

## Rules-based thinking

Rules-based thinking is based on what we 'ought' to do rather than on what will work, and therefore lacks flexibility. Here the argument seems to revolve around a new paradigm, a combination of 'truth *versus* loyalty' and 'justice *versus* mercy'. In this case it is 'truth *versus* justice': in other words, is it more important to be honest in all things than to bring offenders to justice? The resolution here would depend on where, in a hierarchy of moral priorities, we place the two 'goods' of 'tell the truth' and 'catch the wrongdoer'. Both could be argued to fulfil the duty to protect the public; the first from 'official duplicity', and the second from the potential of becoming a victim of crime. This principle, then, is unhelpful here.

## Care-based thinking

Care-based thinking is so flexible that it doesn't provide any robust framework. The level of ethical justification this principle offers depends entirely on who the object of the 'care' should be. If it were the public as potential victims then this principle would justify informer usage. If it is the suspect then it would not. Add to this 'individual *versus* community' paradigm the contention that informer usage eventually erodes social cohesiveness (Parker, 1999) and the 'short-term *versus* long-term' paradigm again becomes an issue.

A perfect system then can only be ethically justified by reference to a utilitarian-based argument suggesting that informer usage is cost-effective and therefore beneficial. Even that however, is not wholly convincing. The Audit Commission's estimate of the cost-effectiveness of informers is grossly overstated (Dunnighan and Norris, 1999), failing to take into account any expense related to running informers and only counting the cash rewards paid out. The training and supervision implications are immense (Dunnighan and Norris, 1996a) and if they were properly addressed service-wide, this expense would further diminish the 'cost-effectiveness' justification. There is also little empirical evidence that proactive policing approaches are any more successful than efficiently managed traditional methods (Bowling, 1999).

Informers can poison communities because communities are built on trust while informers operate on the basis of betrayal (Parker, 1999). England's early twentieth-century class of informers, who received a percentage of the fines levied as a result of their information, eventually caused so much public distaste that bills were submitted to Parliament to curtail their activities on the basis that they produced a 'society cold and selfish' (Parker, 1999). Also there are no 'formal mechanisms, either in law or in police procedure, for limiting the invasion of privacy by police informants' (Dunnighan and Norris, 1999: 82). Thus 'fairness to all' as a guiding principle of policing again sits uneasily with informer usage. When informer usage becomes disproportionate or when informers are seen to 'thrive' (Cooper and Murphy, 1997), the confidence of the courts and public may be lost with dire consequences for society (Dunnighan and Norris, 1999). The greatest weakness, however, is that police guidelines offer no ethical framework for informer usage other than the utilitarian efficiency 'benefits' and access to otherwise inaccessible information (ACPO, 1997). Handlers then are expected to operate in a situation where 'what the law demands, what organisational policy dictates and what their personal ethics require are not always in accord' (Dunnighan and Norris, 1998: 21).

The only ethical justification for a perfect system, then, is one of 'ends' over 'means'. It is clearly challengeable and is too simplistic a stance for modern policing: 'the means by which these ends are achieved are of equal importance in a democratic society' (Dunnighan and Norris, 1999: 84). Consider the effect on this debate of the realities of our current flawed system.

The 'strengths' are quickly dealt with. As the research indicates that abuse is endemic, there can be no rule-based or deontological justification. Neither can there be any care-based justification for a system which coerces and deceives informers, keeps supervisors ignorant (often voluntarily), puts officers at risk of disciplinary action and dupes the courts. The only possible justification is the already vulnerable one of utilitarianism but in this case it is even less substantial. It is based on an argument that it is for the general good of a public whose dual standards allow them to accept that while they wouldn't want us to do it to them, the police can be trusted to only abuse the system when dealing with those who 'deserve it'.

It is necessary now to examine the weaknesses in more detail to appreciate the ethical dilemmas they raise. The most relevant published research was carried out by Dunnighan and Norris between 1993 and 1995. It involved a number of forces, the examination of a very large sample of files, and addressed the views of handlers, controllers and other CID and uniformed officers of varying operational ranks. It can therefore claim to be reasonably generalisable. However, only eleven informers were interviewed so their input was comparatively minor and this will affect the use to which the research is put in this chapter. The abuses that exist in the current system fall into three categories: secrecy, coercion and deception.

## Secrecy

Informers are predominantly handled by detectives who 'develop informal and often unsanctioned strategies for dealing with the risks which arise from... recruiting and running informers' leading to the 'bypassing of organisational and legal controls' (Dunnighan and Norris, 1996: 1). Therefore increased supervisory control will not prevent abuse, as a 'punitive and rule-bound' system is more likely to promote increased secrecy (Norris, 1989), and all the rules aimed at protecting the rights of suspects, public, courts and society rely on official knowledge of the existence and involvement of informers in criminal cases. Moreover, the very definition of informer obscures the coercive nature of their use. Making voluntarism a defining concept 'information given freely' is disingenuous as the vast majority are coerced or even overtly threatened into becoming informers. Eighty four per cent were either in custody or had proceedings against them when recruited, and in 85 per cent of cases the handler initiated discussions about becoming an informer. Interestingly, however, a more recent study (Billingsley, 2000) suggests otherwise. In this a large number of informers were interviewed. There was no evidence that informers had been coerced; on the contrary, their motives were clear and generally involved some personal benefit to themselves.

## Coercion

Handlers assessed the top four motivational factors of informers as; money; concessions regarding charge/sentence/bail; revenge; and help/protection in the future (Dunnighan and Norris, 1996). The evidence does not back up the contention that money is the primary motivator. Payments are relatively small and informers themselves seldom cite money as a motivator (Dunnighan and Norris, 1996). It would appear that handlers, in their assessment of motivation, might be disguising the fact that the chief motivators appear to be coercion and manipulation of power, described by one officer as 'legal blackmail'. Dunnighan and Norris state that 'officers have power over informers because they can translate that power into dependency' (Dunnighan and Norris, 1996: 5) and then describe the three ways that it is done: by 'instrumental', 'informational' and 'affective' means.

## Deception

All three of these strategies rely on deception of some kind. 'Instrumental strategies' involve deceiving the informer under investigation into thinking that only the handler can 'sort out' their situation. The implication is that the handler can do this by deceiving colleagues and supervisors through manipulation of the evidence in order to secure a 'caution' or lesser charge, deceiving the court in the same way and, of course, deceiving the public generally by the use of such tactics. Such deals, even if 'authorised' by a supervisor, are 'informal' and 'outside any judicial scrutiny' (Dunnighan and Norris, 1996: 7). Even where the process is formalised by a letter to the judge in an effort to mitigate on the informers' behalf this just serves to sanction the 'I'll scratch your back if you scratch mine' relationship.

Informational strategies rely on misinforming the informer, usually to increase dependency on the handler as described above. Seventy one per cent of handlers believed that to 'run informers you have to be as devious as they are' (Dunnighan and Norris, 1996: 7). The obvious ethical problem here is that the principle of the suspect being presumed and treated as innocent until proven guilty disappears. All the recent legislation introduced to safeguard the rights of persons in custody (by placing accountability on the custody officer, senior supervisors and the officer in the case) are, in this context, set in direct confrontation with the 'needs' of the organisation to recruit and run more informers on efficiency grounds.

Affective strategies are based on building up a personal relationship with the informer with non-conditional gifts such as cigarettes to 'capitalise on general social rules governing gift relationships and reciprocal obligation' (Dunnighan and Norris, 1996: 8). The ethical dangers here is that these favours continue unofficially outside the custody situation. Thus, 'It is inducements, psychological coercion, deceit and manipulation strategies that are at the heart of securing informers motivational commitment' (Dunnighan and Norris, 1996: 9). These tactics create risks for the handler which inevitably lead to secrecy, which is anathema to the ethical principles of openness and transparency.

Probably the greatest ethical dilemma associated with informers is that those most deeply involved in crime are the most valuable and are generally of no use if they are in custody themselves as a result of their own crimes. Fifty per cent of handlers considered their informers to be immersed in the criminal sub-culture and many admitted 'turning a blind eye' to their activities, allowing them to stay at large when wanted on warrant or even allowing them to profit from their own part in crimes that they informed on. This 'licensing of criminals' has been described as an inevitable consequence of using informers (Dunnighan and Norris, 1996: 13).

Once an informer has been recruited, continued co-operation relies on some kind of reciprocity. Financial reward is not an effective mechanism for this so there cannot be a 'clean' cost-effective justification, i.e. 'you put that cash in and get these results out' as the Audit Commission might like to present matters. The issues are far murkier than that and tainted by 'deals' and deception. Most officers see this reciprocity as a 'necessary evil' (Dunnighan and Norris, 1998: 22). Ethically, this is a lose/lose situation. If the informer benefits from the relationship with the handler that is at least a recognition of the reality of the situation, but it does not stand ethical scrutiny in the broader sense of justice being open and equal for all. If the informer gains no advantage then his recruitment and retention is based on a false promise which is not only unethical but creates an atmosphere in which the informer is virtually forced to deceive and manipulate in order to survive. Not surprising then that there seems little trust in the informer/handler relationship.

The core principle of police evidence in court is that informers should never on any account mislead the court. The use of informers virtually guarantees that this happens regularly, usually on the pretext that current disclosure rules fundamentally contradict the need to protect intelligence sources. Most handlers saw the protection of their informers identity as a 'non-negotiable moral imperative' (Dunnighan and Norris, 1996: 16) and 55 per cent of supervisors did not believe that informers could be run within Home Office guidelines (Dunnighan and Norris, 1996: 20). It should be noted here that new guidelines have recently been introduced to bring working practices in line with the Human Rights Act, 1998.

Some officers then 'are concerned with teasing out the location of the "line" and ensuring they stay on the right side of it. Others know where it is and will cross it when they feel morally justified' (Dunnighan and Norris, 1998: 24). This has been described as a blurring of 'the distinction between what is right and what is lawful' (Cooper and Murphy, 1997: 4) induced by the organisational drive for quality intelligence, the pressure to deliver 'results' and the 'clandestine' nature of informer usage.

So, can informer usage be made ethical or should a modern police service committed to fairness, openness and ethical behaviour abandon the practice altogether? Clearly police leaders have a moral duty to ensure that any system that they expect officers to work within allows them the option of ethical compliance. It cannot be ethical to allow officers to continue working in an area of such moral confusion with only their common sense as a guide. The evidence suggests that even banning the use of informers would not help as their use would simply become unofficial, go 'underground', rely totally on 'deals' rather than money and be even less controllable. In such circumstances, it could be argued that at least an effort to control the system is justifiable on 'ends-based', and 'care-based' grounds. 'Relativism' would even allow an argument for justification on 'rules-based' grounds.

'Ethical relativism' is the acknowledgement that humans develop their beliefs and values within a social context where 'right' and 'wrong' are defined by what is 'best' for that culture (Borchert and Stewart, 1986). The relativist then would say that it is unrealistic to expect there to be a universally accepted way of agreeing what we ought to do; the way each of us selects is derived from our dominant culture. This may offer an explanation of why handlers, operational supervisors, uniformed officers, senior managers, the public, courts, auditors and Home Office all have a different view of the ethics of informer usage; but while ethical relativism offers an attractive alternative to the dogmatism of 'ethical absolutism' it is ultimately unhelpful. The very fact that this doctrine tolerates all views as relevant in their own circumstances makes it useless for trying to base a universal policy upon such an approach.

Cooper and Murphy proffer a solution to the dilemma of competing individual rights: 'following Dworkin we would argue that, as the abrogation of rights is a moral wrong, special grounds are needed for justifying their infringement' (Cooper and Murphy, 1997: 12). They develop Dworkin's theory that where there are competing rights only a 'vivid danger' can justify official infringements of one individual's rights in order to protect another's (Dworkin, 1977: 11). Using more recent work (Bottoms and Brownsword, 1982), they suggest that three criteria might be used to assess this 'vivid danger'. Paraphrased, these are seriousness, frequency and probability. This approach presupposes that the only inducements for informers will be financial and that in every case an accurate assessment of the potential harm and gain can be achieved. Here then is the flaw in this suggestion; it is theoretically sound but practically unworkable. Policing is carried out in 'real time' with incomplete and uncertain information, often supplied by those with an incentive to keep it so. Decisions are most often made at 'ground level' and in a shifting environment. While this model may potentially assist the authorisation of 'participating informant status' (where there is usually time to gather the information and weigh the risks of a particular course of action sufficiently in advance to seek approval from senior management), it will not help with general informer recruitment and running.

One explanation of why the police service continues to use informers is its culture. Stated 'aims and objectives' are an uneasy mix of utilitarian performance indicators and aspirational 'guiding principles'. Where possible, the police strive to attain deontological goals but the majority of operational policing is carried out in a teleological environment where the pressures of increasing demand, decreasing resources, real-time decision-making and the constant juggling of various individuals' competing 'rights' make it virtually impossible to maintain Kantian ideals. In such situations, policing boils down to trying to ensure that the least harm befalls as few people as possible. This is a convoluted version of utilitarianism. As we have already established, this is the only ethical principle that comes close to justifying the use of informers and, in the policing environment, it assumes its own relativist logic.

## Conclusion and recommendations

In conclusion then, it can be argued that there is a possible ethical justification for the use of informers in a modern, professional and accountable police service. However, this justification can only be asserted on utilitarian grounds and largely falls in line with the concepts of 'value for money', 'best value' and the efficient achievement of key performance indicators and quantifiable targets. Even in this limited context, however, it can only be justified if it is carried out not only within the rules and regulations laid down but also entirely within an ethical interpretation of these sometimes ambiguous guidelines. Once these rules are broken or even slightly 'bent' then the utilitarian justification for the police use of informers also becomes unsustainable on ethical grounds.

Formal, documented and strict risk management through fully evaluated training, rigorous supervision and quality assurance systems will be the only way that the police service can continue to practice the use of informers with 'majority public consent' and minimise the chances of further damaging instances of abuse. For this to be achievable the guidelines will need continuous monitoring and updating to ensure that they are clear yet flexible enough to ensure 'ethical compliance'.

It is essential that all these 'safety features' be backed up by the kind of integrity testing pioneered by the Metropolitan Police and now gradually spreading across the service. In such an environment, officers in high risk areas such as informer handling are not only targeted as a result of complaints or suspicions but are likely to be 'tested' at random, at some point in their work. Such an environment has the best chance available at present of both preventing susceptible officers from abusing the system (whether for corrupt or misguided motives) and of assisting ethical officers to operate effectively without fear of unintentionally offending or being tainted by unethical colleagues.

Greater use could also be made of ethics panels, analogous to ethics committees in universities to which certain kinds of research or experiments must be submitted for approval. These committees use academics unconnected with the proposed study to specifically address ethical issues. Their decision is binding. The police service would benefit from greater of use 'ethics panels' in order to test and quality assure informer handling proposals.

The increasing use of surveillance technology available to Chief Constables as a result of recent legislation may expose an unexpected level of corruption in provincial forces. Operations are riskier if they rely on intelligence from the informer alone. It will be important that the informer handling management plan ensures there is significant use of covert surveillance equipment. This gets closer to the informer operating within a controlled environment and provides a degree of accountability that has been lacking.

This discussion has supported the use of informers in law enforcement on a utilitarian basis, subject to safeguards that are sufficiently effective to ensure support by the public and from the courts. It has highlighted the urgent need for ethical and realistic professional standards guidance to provide a framework within which informers and agents can be employed. Judging by past experience, guidance on its own is unlikely to succeed without an effective management programme determined to change the organisational culture which has led to so many past embarrassments. Unless this happens, for the reasons we have discussed in this chapter, history will repeat itself with further revelations of unprincipled informer handling. This will erode the credibility of the service and lead to the curtailment of use of informers.

# References

Alderson, J. (1999) *Principled Policing. Protecting the public with integrity*, Winchester: Waterside Press.

Association of Chief Police Officers, Crime Committee (1997), 'Guidelines on the use and management of informants'.

Association of Chief Police Officers and HM Customs and Excise (1999), *Public Statement on Standards in Covert Law Enforcement Techniques*, London: HMSO.

Audit Commission, Report (1993), *Helping With Enquiries: Tackling crime effectively*, London: HMSO.

Audit Commission, Report (1996), *Detecting a Change*, London: HMSO.

Billingsley, R. (2000), 'An examination of the relationship between informers and their handlers in England', unpublished Ph.D thesis, Loughborough University.

Bloom, S. (1999), 'Readings in Ethics', Strategic command course ethical fitness seminar run by the Institute for Global Ethics, 4 June.

Borchert, D.M. and Stewart, D. (1986), 'Exploring Ethics', cited in Bloom (1999): 91–107.

Bottoms, A.E. and Brownsword, R. (1982), cited in Cooper and Murphy (1997).

Bowling, B. (1999), Address to the Strategic command course on 'Researching Informers, Surveillance and Intel', 10 May.

Charman, S. and Savage, S. (1999) 'New Politics of Law and Order: Labour Crime and Justice' in Powell, M. (ed) *New Labour, New Welfare State*? Bristol: Policy Press

Clavell, J. (1981), *The Art of War by Sun Tzu*, London: Hodder & Stoughton.

Cooper, P. and Murphy, J. (1997), 'Ethical approaches for police officers when working with informants in the development of criminal intelligence in the UK', *Journal of Social Policy*, 26 (1): 1–20.

Cox, B., Shirley, J. and Short, M. (1977) *The Fall of Scotland Yard*, London: Penguin Books.

Davis, N. (1999). 'Dispatches' television documentary broadcast, 18 March 1999.

Dunnighan, C. and Norris, C. (1996a), 'A risky business: the recruitment and running of informers by English police officers', *Police Studies*, Vol. 19, no 2: 1–25.

Dunnighan, C. and Norris, C. (1996b), 'The nark's game', *New Law Journal*. Vol. 146, 22 and 29 March.

Dunnighan, C. and Norris, C. (1998), 'Some ethical dilemmas in the handling of police informers', *Public Money and Management* Jan–Mar: 21–25.

Dunnighan, C. and Norris, C. (1999), 'The detective, the snout and the Audit Commission: the real costs in using informants', *Howard Journal*, Vol. 38, no 1, Feb: 67–86.

Dworkin, R. (1977), cited in Cooper and Murphy (1997).

Her Majesty's Inspector of Constabulary (1996), *Post-sentence Interviews with Persons Serving Custodial Sentences*. Home Office Circular, 22 July.

Her Majesty's Inspector of Constabulary (1999), *Police Integrity: Securing and maintaining public confidence*. Home Office.

Kleinig, J. (1996), *The Ethics of Policing*, Cambridge: Cambridge University Press.

Kidder, R.M. (1992), 'How good people make tough choices', cited in Bloom (1999): 71–89.

Kidder, R.M. (1994), 'Shared values for a troubled world', cited in Bloom (1999): 31–38.

MacPherson, Sir William (1999), *Report of the Stephen Lawrence Inquiry*. Cm 4262–I, London: The Stationery Office Ltd.

Metropolitan Police, *Commissioner's Annual Report for 1983*, by Sir Robert Mark, London: HMSO.

Norris, C. (1989), 'Avoiding trouble: the patrol officer's perception of the public', cited in Dunnighan and Norris (1996a).

Parker, G. (1999), Address to the Strategic Command course on 'The dangers of informer-based social control', 10 May.

Phillips, D. (1999), Address to the Strategic Command Course on Intelligence-led Policing, 11 May.

Raine, J.W. and Wilson, M.J. (1995), 'New public management and criminal justice', *Public Money and Management*, Jan–Mar: 35–40.

Smith, D.J. (1983), *Police and Public in London 1. A survey of Londoners*. London: Policy Studies Institute.

Williamson, T. M. (1990), 'Strategic changes in police interrogation: an examination of police and suspect behaviour in the Metropolitan Police in order to determine the effects of new legislation, technology and organisational policies', unpublished Ph. D thesis, University of Kent.

Woodcock, Sir John, Her Majesty's Chief Inspector of Constabulary (1992), 'Trust in the Police – the search for truth', IPEC '92. Metropolitan Police Library, London.

# 4 Informers, agents and accountability:
## some matters arising from the use of human information sources by the Police and the Security Service

## Nigel South

'Humint', i.e. reliance on human information sources as opposed to technological surveillance/probing is essential both for political intelligence and police investigations. What it is intended for, how it is used, to whom it is available marks the difference.

(Blum and Ricks, 1996: 21)

## Introduction

This chapter is concerned with the use of informers by the police and of agents by the Security Service, in England and Wales. It discusses definitions and motives of police informers and of agents recruited by the Security Service, and the extent to which their use and management may be held accountable. Broad issues relating to accountability are reviewed, including questions about the ethics and the effectiveness, or otherwise, of using informers and agents. The conclusion calls for the degree of reasonable openness about these matters which might be expected in a liberal democracy. The theme of the argument throughout this chapter is that as the police and Security Service ask for public and Parliamentary support in their use of (and increasing reliance upon) human information sources, the *quid pro quo* must be that they provide the public and Parliament with surer guarantees of probity and of adherence to mechanisms designed to enhance accountability.

In an open society, research on such a key but little understood area of the activities of the police and Security Service should be self-evidently desirable but may often face obstacles arising from the sensitivity and confidentiality of the subject. This chapter draws upon original and literature-based research conducted between the late 1980s and 1999[1] and the focus is on practices and issues arising in England.

## Police informers and Security Service agents

### Police informers

One starting-point for the assessment of the significance and accountability (or otherwise) of the use of police informers is to outline the different types of informant. Dorn *et al* (1992: 123-127) suggest a number of informant types derived from their research in England. For example, there is the 'public-spirited' informant who may be either genuinely well-intentioned or malicious and self-serving; the 'police buff' who over-identifies with police officers – and probably supplies information of little value; and the 'professional informant' who may be seeking a reward or, if facing trial, the preparation of a confidential 'text' (i.e. letter) that will indicate to the Judge that the informant has been of assistance in a police investigation (*ibid*: 126-7).

In certain cases, active criminals as well as both 'organisational' and 'general public' sources, may seek the status of being a 'police informant' in order to strike up and maintain a relationship with police officers (cf Ericson, 1981: 122; Harney and Cross, 1960). There may be various reasons for this, for example – as a utilitarian investment, to create a friendship that may be called upon by the informant when facing legal or other problems; or an over-identification with the general police role or an individual officer. The potential dangers and scope for relationships stepping well beyond the bounds of control and accountability are obvious here.

With regard to the 'running' or 'handling' of informers, some skills and techniques involved in recruiting and cultivating contacts, arranging meetings and handling difficult situations, are often jealously guarded by police officers and treated as confidential matters of arcane 'insider' knowledge. In fact, there are probably few techniques which factual and fictional media have not already detailed somewhere in the huge amount of entertainment and documentary output concerned with modern police practice.[2] Nonetheless, the attempt to preserve a sense of occupational secrecy and mystique around informer handling can also be seen to send a clear 'hands off' message to those viewed as meddlesome and interfering. The implications for provision of oversight and organisational demands for accountability are that rules and regulations may be 'seen' – officers are aware of them – but 'not heard', i.e. they are ignored. I shall return later to this point, and the distinction between 'idealised accountability' that may be pursued by putting impressive-sounding policies and rules in place *versus* 'real accountability' which may – in practice – be actively resisted or, more passively, simply avoided and ignored.

## The security service and informers as 'agents'[3]

There have been many historical studies of the use of infiltrators in political movements. Similarly, there are innumerable well- to ill-informed fictional accounts of the trade of spies and intelligence officers. However, there has been little academic research (at least in the UK) on the use of informers – or 'agents' as they are termed in this milieu – by the domestic intelligence agency. This body is popularly referred to as MI5 but is more properly titled the Security Service. A recent thawing of some of the icy secrecy surrounding this agency has resulted in more open discussion of its activities and methods (Rimington, 1994a). This development fits with the new role the Security Service has sought since the end of the Cold War and its involvement, first, in anti-terrorist activity and, more recently, in work against serious organised crime and drug trafficking (provided for under s.1 of the Security Services Act 1996).[4] As Blum and Ricks (1996: 17) observe, the post-Cold War context has seen widespread 'expansion of previously political intelligence agencies into fighting international, organised economic (entrepreneurial) crime' and has been noted as an international development. This has raised new questions and concerns about the operations and accountability of political intelligence agencies (see *ibid*: 17-31).

Unlike the police who often recruit informers in the course of crime investigations and detention of suspects, the Security Service is not an enforcement agency with powers of arrest or detention.[5] Representatives of the Security Service interviewed in 1996 asserted that they tended to be more interested in gathering intelligence on organisations than on individuals *per se*[6] and that recruitment of agents is accomplished through either direct approach to individuals or via individuals volunteering their services. It is clear from the earlier outline of types of police informers that a certain caution is advisable about those who put themselves forward as volunteers. Nonetheless the Security Service officers interviewed suggested that in the work and world of the Security Service, volunteer sources may often make the best agents.

While the new Security Service 'Glasnost'[7] acknowledges use of certain procedures and 'tradecraft', matters relating to the minutiae and identifying characteristics of any operations and cases of recruitment are not open to discussion (Rimington, 1994b). For the Security Service there is an understandable and emphatic claim that maximum secrecy and professional discretion are imperative in their use of agents. On the other hand, for critics and even sympathetic reformers, a case can be made for a greater degree of transparency, which need not produce any operational risks but could provide for more penetrating scrutiny of what the Security Service and its operatives and agents actually do.[8] Ideally, such scrutiny should be double-edged and have the capacity to identify what the Security Service does *not* do but should, and activities that it *does* engage in but should not! On the one hand, this may mean reviewing tasks that should be pursued in the interests of national security and public safety but which are not currently undertaken, and reviewing on the other hand, the pursuit of surveillance and intelligence gathering against groups undertaken for unjustifiable reasons. The case of David Shayler, a former Security Service officer turned 'whistleblower' has raised a number of relevant issues, rekindling calls from critics for greater scrutiny. Also recently, in 1999, past and current government ministers who are ordinarily supportive of the Service, were angered by its failure to inform them about the identification of several British citizens as former Eastern bloc agents, leaving them to learn of the revelations in the Sunday newspapers.

The case for accountability, scrutiny and enhanced oversight of Security Service use of agents is a strong one, and the same applies to the police regarding their use of informers. If society allows enforcement and intelligence agencies to employ covert agents, the *quid pro quo* should be mechanisms of accountability and overview which mean that mistakes are not covered up, excesses do not go uncorrected, and that Parliament receives honest reporting on the actions undertaken in its name.

## The use and accountability of informers and agents in a democratic society

The role of the informer is one of ambiguous status and those who provide information to the authorities may be applauded and celebrated, feared or derided. In one oft-quoted remark, J. Edgar Hoover suggested that 'unlike the totalitarian practice, the informant in America serves of his own free will, fulfilling one of the citizenship obligations of our democratic form of government' (Harney and Cross, 1960: 18; Ericson, 1981: 133). During the McCarthy hearings of the 1950s, testimony before the House Un-American Activities Committee was deemed patriotic (Navasky, 1980). In more recent years, 'penitent' major criminals informing on organised crime in the US or Italy (Falcone, 1993) as well as the 'supergrasses' in Britain in the 1970s (Campbell, 1994; Greer, 1995), achieved both notoriety and celebrity. In Nazi Germany the informer was a feared secret agent of the repressive state (Weyrauch, 1986), while in English history, the informer was once a vilified but nonetheless key instrument of moral, fiscal and legal surveillance (Beresford, 1958; South, 1987).

## Guidelines, rules and prescription of practice: governing the police use of informers

The first set of guidelines were distributed by the Home Office in Circular 97, 1969 and concerned 'Informants who take part in crime'. These have only recently been replaced with the Association of Chief Police Officers' (ACPO) 'National Guidelines on the Use and Management of Informants', and more recently still by codes of practice produced to ensure compatability with the Human Rights Act, 1998. The effectiveness of these latter developments is as yet unknown, but recent research (Dunnighan and Norris, 1996, a, b), as well as earlier work by Maguire and Norris (1992), suggest that such guidelines are not easily translated into faithful practice. The issue of training and advice for those working with informers has been another area receiving insufficient attention until relatively recently (South, 1995). The ACPO Guidelines aim to promote some national uniformity in training and practice, contributing to greater internal accountability within the hierarchy of police supervision. They also prescribe practice regarding access to information; the security of identities; and rewarding informers. Nonetheless, all of these procedures may still simply be ignored. As Dunnighan and Norris (1996 a, b) found, the rules and guidelines exist and officers are made aware of them, yet in their study these same officers routinely broke the rules and ignored the guidelines; and these findings were confirmed by Billingsley (2000) in a later study.

## Accountability and ethical issues in the use of informers

The Audit Commission (1993: para. 86) remarked that 'in some forces there is a disinclination to use [informants] because of ethical problems – informants may have close connections to the criminal activities for which they are receiving information payments'. To some police officers it is a matter of principle that criminals should not be rewarded for their association with criminal activities. In an early and influential article on this topic, Oscapella (1980: 144) noted that the use of incentives to encourage informers to co-operate may, in some circumstances, 'be wholly improper, both morally and legally.... The 'licensing' of... minor offences might not seem offensive, but it becomes increasingly unacceptable with the progressive seriousness of the crime being ignored. 'Some officers find the use of informers ethically distasteful because it represents 'dirty work'. The view here is that informers themselves are untrustworthy and tainted, and that reliance on them can, in turn, taint and corrupt police work.

In several studies, including my own earlier work (South, 1995), it is observed that some objectors to the use of informers feel the main ethical issue is that 'co-operation' is often elicited by putting some form of pressure on the potential informer, often when they are in a particularly vulnerable position and state of mind. Ideally, the guiding principle ought to be that informers should not be *coerced* into working for the police or the Security Service. In practice, it is widely acknowledged that in varying ways, pressures which may amount to coercion are frequently brought to bear (on deals, inducements and threats generally, see Maguire and

Norris, 1992: 47-48; on pressures on informants, Ericson, 1981: chapter 5).
This cannot usually be regarded as ethical. Further, if coercion is routine
does this demonstrate a failure of accountable practice or condoning of
coercion by the oversight process? The potential for fudging the issue is
apparent though – when does 'a request' become 'encouragement',
become 'pressure', become 'coercion'? Interestingly, a later study
(Billingsley, 2000) where 120 informers were interviewed throughout
England, failed to identify any suggestion of coercion; on the contrary,
their motives were mostly to secure a benefit for themselves, not
necessarily financial.

The personal agenda of an informer, possibly leading to what
Oscapella (1980: 144) calls 'selective informing', thereby influencing the
direction of police activity, also has implications for accountable and
ethical practice. Police can guard against such 'steering' but, at the same
time, they may be unlikely to refuse to accept good information (whether
they subsequently act on useful information is a different matter). Turning
this point around, there are also accountability, ethical and other
dimensions to the police use of informers in selectively targeting certain
individuals or groups. This could, for example, lead to accusations of
persecution and harassment, or racial discrimination. The latter has
become an acutely sensitive area for police work following the
Macpherson Report (1999) (see below). There may also be concerns raised
by and for police officers when it comes to the targeting of individuals
with criminal connections with the aim of 'turning' and recruiting them,
because the methods employed may seem unpalatable. Policy, training
and supervision must be clear about how such matters are dealt with. For
example, when (if ever) do persistent attempts to recruit an informer
become unjustifiable harassment?

## Rights and citizenship, ethics and accountability

A number of the primary issues in this area have been examined in an
article co-authored by a lecturer in police management and a serving
superintendent. Cooper and Murphy (1997) seek to develop the 'basis for
an ethical model of informer handling' (*ibid*: 1) and conclude that a 'rights
based approach' would restrict manipulative coercion and enhance the
principle of voluntarism in relation to informants (*ibid*: 17). As this
important area of the work of the police and Security Service continues to
expand, it will receive greater scrutiny in the future and practices must
demonstrably be underpinned by sound judgement and justification. The
discourse of citizenship rights is of growing importance and now enforced
by supranational courts within the judicial framework of the European
Union. Further, the new 1998 Human Rights Act brings into UK law (from
2000) provisions of the European Convention on Human Rights and will
be an additional strong source of support for rights-based criticisms of the

non-accountable or abusive use of powers by state agencies. As Cooper and Murphy (1997: 17-18) remark:

> a rights based approach... has the capacity to focus official attention on the idea of the citizen as a person to whom the police service owes fundamental duties, which the pursuit of criminal intelligence cannot override.

## Accountability and utility

Broadly speaking, policing is being geared to more proactive styles of work (Reiner, 1994). Some reflection of this was found in the 1993 Audit Commission report *Helping with Enquiries* which discussed and made recommendations concerning effective crime management. One key element of this report was the view that informers 'offer a very cost-effective source of detections' (paragraph 84), and the recommendation that detectives should be encouraged 'to cultivate informants' who should then be 'tasked to produce information on high priority crimes or criminals. Forces should also review the current budgets for informers and ensure that officers are aware of the cost-efficiency of informers' (paragraph 130). This was a strong endorsement by an influential Government agency of the use of informers as part of proactive and intelligence-fed/-led policing. However, such assertions, while perhaps persuasive in their own terms, should also be critically appraised in other ways.

Dunnighan and Norris (1996b: 457; 1999) undertook the most recent detailed study of the use of informers in several police forces in England and provided an analysis concerning the actual costs associated with use of informers and incurred through recruitment and cultivation, contact, and supervision. Their conclusions are starkly at odds with those of the Audit Commission and they suggest that 'highly dubious claims are being made about the cost-effectiveness of informers'. In short, this study concluded that 'the effectiveness of informers in clearing up crime is seriously overstated'. By contrast, in his Toronto study, Ericson (1981: 127) argued that, 'Taking [a] broad definition of informant... and the key role of information production in the making of detective cases, we argue that informants are central to detective work.'

It remains reasonable to query and attempt to clarify whether, *in practice*, informers actually do deliver information that clears up crime, and indeed whether officers who say they find informers essential, actually do use them. In general, the literature and the interviews in my own study (South, 1995) suggest the following propositions:

(a) Where informers are registered and their information is properly graded as to its quality, then high-grade information does lead to prevention of crime or arrests of offenders – *when that information is acted upon*. It was acknowledged in interviews that for various reasons – poor liaison, pressure of work, time off, etc. – even high-grade information may not always be acted upon. Hence, the contribution of information from informers to crime clear-up rates may well have potential, but this may not be realised in practice.

(b) Lower-grade information might still prove useful background intelligence in building profiles of crimes or offenders, but how successful this is will largely depend upon whether the information is passed on in appropriate ways and how effective and well established local and force intelligence offices are (Maguire and John, 1995).

(c) Overall, several estimates offered by police forces in my own study suggest that informer-generated material plays a relatively small but nonetheless significant part in dealing with a broad range of crimes, especially those classed as serious. However, it is important to place this observation in the wider context of how crimes are 'solved'. Various studies have shown that most crimes are cleared up as the result of members of the public (usually the victim or a witness) providing vital information to the police as soon as they arrive at the scene of the crime (Reiner, 1992: 151). This accounts for the 'solving' of a great deal of crime. For the remainder, however, the chances are that either the crime will not be solved or that another source of information will be required to provide a direction for investigation. It can be here that informers – while contributing to *relatively* few cases overall – may make important contributions to the clear-up of crimes where the police have no other lead. As Ericson (1981: 127) observes in his Toronto study, 'If suspects were not initially known in a case, the only significant hope available to detectives to achieve a clearance was to find and create an informant to assist them.' Here though it should also be noted that the imperative Ericson reports, 'to identify or suggest *possible* suspects', is potentially a key element of the kinds of case-making and prosecution that have led to a disastrous and dismaying sequence of miscarriages of justice in the UK in recent years (Walker and Starmer, 1993).

(d) Despite their evident value to some officers, working with criminal informers is not at all attractive to others. Having good informers may make a good detective (although not necessarily), but a good detective may still be good even without any informers (although detectives do need information). In some contexts of police practice and prevailing strategy, there may be an *expected* use of informers (perhaps because of the enthusiasm of some senior officer) and hence much talk of their value and utilisation. However, it may be that this is not met by the reality of practice. Where there is a reluctance to use informants and agents this may be for very good reasons. Such reasons should not be ignored for the sake of accountancy-led arguments about cost-effectiveness. As Dunnighan and Norris (1999: 67) recently noted, 'as the reality of using informers raises profound ethical problems there is a danger that an increase in their use could further undermine police legitimacy'.

## Accountability: ideal versus real?

There is a sense in which we might well be able to move toward an 'ideal' state of formal accountability in this area, as measured by rules and policies. However, whether this would be translated into real practice by police informer handlers and runners of Security Service agents is quite a different question. We must therefore consider the issue of accountability in terms of informal occupational culture as well as at the formal 'rules and policy' level (in the absence of information about the occupational culture of the Security Service, the following focuses on police work).

Police accountability always faces the problem of balancing strict application of rules with the need to allow operational flexibility. This is generally accepted within reasonable limits. However, such limits may be unacceptably stretched by the informal police 'canteen culture' and invocation of the fictitious 'Ways and Means Act' as a form of justification. The study of the Metropolitan Police undertaken by the Policy Studies Institute in the early 1980s (Smith and Gray, 1983) found evidence of disturbing levels of racism and sexual discrimination (still a problem according to recent reports of Her Majesty's Inspector of Constabulary in 1996, 1998 and the 1999 Macpherson Report).

The PSI report did not explicitly explore the matter of informant use and management but as the classic investigation of the ways in which British police culture facilitates police deviance and the negotiation of rules, avoiding forms of managerial calling to account, the report is worth revisiting. The authors distinguished between three types of 'rule' within police culture: the 'working', the 'inhibitory' and the 'presentational' (Smith and Gray, 1983: 169–72). The first type represents the 'accepted' way of working but is by no means always in line with formal regulations. Inhibitory rules are formal rules which carry organisational weight and must therefore be followed, even if seen as unnecessary by officers. Presentational rules highlight the disparity between how the police are supposed to act and how they actually act. As Reiner (1996: 730) summarises, 'Presentational rules are those official rules which have no bearing on police practice, but which nonetheless provide the terms in which accounts after the event must be couched.' While regulations and reporting practices concerning informer handling have arguably been tightened up since the introduction of the ACPO guidelines, police sources acknowledge that resistance to management supervision and public accountability remain strong features of the occupational culture. The recent shameful evidence provided by the Macpherson Inquiry report, shows that despite the efforts of many, and recommendations of earlier reports from Scarman onward, police culture continues to reproduce racism and sexism. It is therefore unsurprising if less visible police deviance is harder to regulate.

A key moment in the development of 'formal level' accountability and openness in this area came in 1994 when the BBC televised the Dimbleby Lecture (13 June, 1994) delivered by Mrs Stella Rimington, then Director-General of the Security Service. In her talk and published text, Mrs Rimington observed that 'Accountability lies at the heart of the tension between liberty and security' (1994a: 11). Accepting aspects of Mrs Rimington's arguments but being cautious about other claims, I argue that it is acceptable and inevitable that the use of informants and agents will be treated as a matter of secrecy and security. However, the police and security services must accept that for society to be able to have faith in the propriety of actions undertaken under such conditions, then accountability must be real and demonstrable.

Furthermore, if the use of informers (and related techniques such as undercover operations) are to become an even more central feature of criminal investigation and Security Service work, then society needs to be better educated about the implications of such a strategy. This might be advanced through the publication of proceedings of inquiries, minutes of public watchdog committees and so on. In this respect, it is noteworthy that in Australia, the New South Wales Police and the Independent Commission Against Corruption released a *public* edition of their joint *New South Wales Police Informant Management Plan* (see *Australian Law Journal*, 1994: 493); and in Canada, the background research documents and report relating to the police use of informers, of the *Board of Inquiry on Activities of the RCMP Related to Allegations Made in the Senate of Canada* (1991: Ottawa), were also published in the public domain. Requirements of greater openness about the rationale supporting use of informants and agents, and the procedures and rules that are in place, could promote cultural change within the police and Security Service organisations. This could, in turn, move them away from the secrecy and mystique surrounding informants that has led to so many problems in the past. Such openness could also lead to a more informed realism on the part of the public about the issues at stake. The latter objective should be of value to the relevant agencies as well as to the benefit of democracy.

## Conclusions

One of the key unresolved issues in the area in relation to accountability and justice is the tension between the need for transparency *versus* dispute over the disclosure of evidence in a court trial. This generally hinges on the arguments that, on the one hand, withholding of prosecution evidence from the defence can evidently lead to miscarriages of justice, *versus* the proposition that such disclosure would lead to the identification of the informer and place them in danger. This is a fundamental aspect of the overall problem of accountability. On the one hand, justice and the courts might reasonably expect that evidence submitted be open to further questioning; on the other hand, courts are also likely to accept the arguments of prosecution and police that sources must be protected in 'the public interest'. In various jurisdictions, including the UK, there have been recent initiatives to try to resolve these tensions (Home Office, 1995). Nonetheless, the problem remains.

The 'bottom line' is that the use of informers and agents is not going to diminish; indeed the premium placed on intelligence gathering is only likely to increase. Where uncertainty arises is how society should respond to this trend, and, in turn, how police and the Security Service should and will respond to the legitimate concerns of democratic accountability.

## Notes

1 See the historical review of the employment of private agents, including the early informers, in South, 1987; use of informants in drugs law enforcement is reported in Dorn, Murji and South, 1992. Some of the material presented here on police use of informants is derived from an unpublished report prepared by South (1995) for the Police Research Group, Home Office, London. I am grateful to the PRG for supporting that research and to Barry Webb and various anonymous referees for checking and correcting aspects of this report. A summary of some findings and issues can be found in Greer and South, 1998. The section of this paper concerning the Security Service's (MI5) use of informants as 'agents' is derived from collaborative work with Dr Steven Greer, Faculty of Law, University of Bristol, our interview and correspondence with the Security Service, and the draft of a paper Dr Greer prepared on this subject. In 1999, during preparation of this paper, two senior police officers offered further observations on the use of informants and the accountability process.

2 Or, of course, the spy trade. In his overview of 'intelligence power in peace and war', Herman (1996: 324) observes: 'Even Humint – the least technological form of collection [of intelligence] – now has its highly developed tradecraft', and cites Kuzichkin (1990), as a thorough account of KGB training.

3 I am grateful here to Steven Greer for permission to draw upon his draft paper summarising our interview with Security Service personnel.

4 In relation to developments in intelligence-led policing during the 1990s, it is worth noting that this change of role for the Security Service has occurred alongside, first, the consolidation of various disparate police intelligence data bases under the National Criminal Intelligence Service, and more recently, the creation (under the 1997 Police Act) of a new, operational, National Crime Squad. All of this creates a powerful new set of 'police/security' agencies with legitimate powers to 'burgle and bug', but with limited accountability to Parliament or the public. See South, 1998.

5 Farson (1991: 66) describes the two general models underpinning arrangements for domestic intelligence gathering: the British, dividing domestic security activity between the Security Service and police Special Branches, and the US model which gives the FBI 'a joint mandate to conduct criminal and national security investigations'. See also Lustgarten and Leigh, 1994.

6 Note however that independent commentators and former Security Service officers have emphasised that the Service does maintain numerous files on individuals, including members of the main political parties (BBC2 *Newsnight*, 26 August, 1997).

7 The context in which permission to conduct the interview I draw upon was granted. Steven Greer and I once again express our thanks to the members of the Service who offered this access.

8 Herman's (1996: 326) book on the UK intelligence community has only one index entry for 'accountability': this is used in a sub-section headed 'Environment' and refers to the location of the intelligence services within Government bureaucracy, Treasury constraints, and the need to avoid causing political embarrassment to the Government.

# References

Audit Commission (1993) *Helping with Enquiries: tackling crime effectively*, London: HMSO.

Beresford, M. (1958), 'The common informers, the penal statutes and economic regulation', *Economic History Review*, 2, 2: 221-38.

Billingsley, R. (2000), 'An examination of the relationship between informers and their handlers within the police service in England', unpublished Ph.D thesis, Loughborough University.

Blum, R. and Ricks, M. (1996), 'Political intelligence agencies acting against organised international economic crime: potentials, problems, forecasts', *Journal of Financial Crime*, 4, 1: 17-31.

Campbell, D. (1994) *The Underworld*, London: BBC Books.

Cooper, P. and Murphy, J. (1997) 'Ethical approaches for police officers when working with informants in the development of criminal intelligence in the United Kingdom', *Journal of Social Policy*, 26, 1: 1-20.

Dunnighan, C. and Norris, C. 1996, 'The nark's game' (parts 1 and 2), *New Law Journal*, 22 March: 402-404, and 29 March: 456-457.

Dunnighan, C. and Norris, C. (1999) 'The detective, the snout and the Audit Commission: the real costs in using informants', *The Howard Journal of Criminal Justice*, 38, 1: 67-86.

Dorn, N. Murji, K. and South, N. (1992) *Traffickers: Drug markets and law enforcement*, London: Routledge.

Ericson, R. (1981) *Making Crime: A study of detective work*, Toronto: Butterworths.

Falcone, G. (1993) *Men of Honour: the truth about the mafia*, London: Warner Books.

Farson, S. (1991) 'Security intelligence *versus* criminal intelligence', *Policing and Society*, 2: 65-87.

Greer, S. (1995) *Supergrasses*, Oxford: Clarendon Press.

Greer, S. and South, N. (1998) 'The criminal informant: police management, supervision and control' in S. Field and C. Pelser (eds.) *Invading the Private? New investigative methods in Europe*, Aldershot: Ashgate.

Harney, M. and Cross, J. (1960; 1968, 2nd edn) *The Informer in Law Enforcement*, Springfield, Ill.: Charles Thomas.

HMCIC (Her Majesty's Chief Inspector of Constabulary) (1996, 1998) *Annual Reports*, London: The Stationery Office.

Herman, M. (1996) *Intelligence Power in Peace and War*, Cambridge: Cambridge University Press.

Home Office (1995) *Disclosure: a consultation document*, Cmnd. 2864, London: HMSO.

Kuzichkin, V. (1990) *Inside the KGB: Myth and reality*, London: Deutsch.

Lustgarten, L. and Leigh, I. (1994) *In from the Cold: National security and Parliamentary democracy*, Oxford: Clarendon Press.

Macpherson Report (1999) *Report of the Macpherson Inquiry*, London: The Stationery Office.

Maguire, M. and John, T, 1995, *Intelligence, Surveillance and Informants: Integrated approaches*, Police Research Group, London: Home Office.

Maguire, M. and Norris, C. (1992) *The Conduct and Supervision of Criminal Investigations*, Royal Commission on Criminal Justice, Research Study 5, London: HMSO.

Navasky, V. 1980, *Naming Names*, New York: Viking.

Oscapella, E. (1980) 'A study of informers in England', *Criminal Law Review*: 136-146.

Reiner, R. (1992) *The Politics of the Police*, Hemel Hempstead: Harvester.

Reiner, R. (1996) 'Policing and the police' in M. Maguire *et al* (eds) *The Oxford Handbook of Criminology*, Oxford: Oxford University Press.

Rimington, S. (1994a) *Security and Democracy: Is there a conflict?* (The Richard Dimbleby Lecture, 1994) London: BBC Education.

Rimington, S. (1994b) 'Intelligence, security and the law', The James Smart Lecture, James Smart Council, Edinburgh: Scottish Office.

Smith, D. and Gray, J. (1983) *The Police in Action*, London: Policy Studies Institute / Aldershot: Gower.

South, N. 1987, 'Law, profit and "private persons": private and public policing in English history' in C. Shearing and P. Stenning (eds) *Private Policing*, Sage: Beverly Hills.

South, N. (1995) 'The police use of informants', unpublished report to Police Research Group, Home Office.

South, N. (1998) 'The police and policing' in I. Budge *et al* (eds) *The New British Politics*, Addison Wesley Longman: Harlow.

Walker, C. and Starmer, K. (eds) (1993) *Justice in Error*, London: Blackstone.

Weyrauch, W. O. 1986, 'Gestapo informants: facts and theory of undercover operations', *Columbia Journal of Transnational Law*, 24: 553-96.

# 5 Informers' careers: motivations and change

## Roger Billingsley

## Introduction

This chapter examines informers' motives for giving information and the reasons why they become involved. It addresses the need for law enforcement agencies to examine their relationships with informers, and the importance of managing an informer's motives. More importantly, this chapter will focus on motivational change with informers, and the implications of such changes to law enforcement policy makers.

The police service in the United Kingdom has a long history of using informers successfully, and has argued consistently for their continued use as an investigative tool in the fight against crime. At the same time, increasing evidence has emerged suggesting that the use of informers can create unethical police practices, short-cuts in the criminal justice system, or could even be instrumental in the miscarriage of justice. In addition, law enforcement agencies throughout the world are facing civil litigation where informers have been used. Specifically, it is becoming common-place for individuals who have become involved with the police, to complain that they have not been afforded sufficient 'duty of care'.

This concern is particularly relevant to the informer, and will become even more apparent following the implementation of new legislation in October 2000, which will require all public authorities, including the police, to ensure that what they do is compatible with an individual's rights (Human Rights Act, 1998). For example, every person has a right to privacy and a right to a fair trial. These two issues alone will inevitably have an impact on the use of informers. As a result, the police service will need to look far more closely at its relationships with informers. It will also have to learn more about the implications arising from the police/informer partnership.

Historically, the police have tended to rely on guidance provided by a Home Office Circular (Home Office, 1969) and only then after the Home Secretary expressed his concern regarding the lack of police control of informers who were participating in crime. The police service struggled on for nearly thirty years, using only this advisory document, until the Association of Chief Police Officers commissioned more detailed Guidelines for the police service (ACPO, 1995). This became the standard set of rules for police forces throughout the United Kingdom, although these rules have been subject to regular amendment.

More recently, the police service have accepted the need to publish a code of practice (ACPO, 1999) for operational covert policing tactics, which includes the use of informers. This code covers a number of important issues generally, but does not refer specifically to the relationship between the informer and handler, and no mention is made of the informers' motives for giving information.

There is now some evidence that law enforcement agencies in the United Kingdom as well as North America have recognised the need to improve the way they manage and control their informers. One important precondition to this is to examine the so-called motivational factors involved, in particular to examine the reasons why informers give information to the police. Agencies have now begun to realise they can control informers only after they have learnt more about them, especially about the reasons which led them to inform in the first place. Thus Hanvey (1995) identified the need for handlers to examine the motives of an informer as necessary because, 'the reason why a person is providing the information is a powerful factor in directing and maintaining control of the informant'.

Having recognised that 'To understand the motive of an informant is to have the key to the control of the informant' (Brown, 1985), the police service accepted there was a need to establish the motives of informers in order for them to use and control them fully. Indeed, Ericson (1993) went further, suggesting that if a motive was not apparent, the police officer should create one so that the informer has a purpose which can be ultimately satisfied. There has been little support from others for such a view, and most agree that an informer will always have a reason of their own and that reason needs to be established.

## A look at some of the existing literature

The literature on informers' motives is somewhat sparse and most research to date has tended to rely on data obtained from law enforcement officers, rather than from informers themselves. This may be understandable, given the sensitivity and nature of the informers business, but the findings can hardly be regarded as satisfactory. Previous work has tended to concentrate on identifying reasons why informers are prepared to give information. This is not sufficient if the police are to improve their management skills. They need to understand that motives may change, and that such changes are bound to affect the relationship they have with informers. That said, the previous studies do provide a foundation on which to build, and provide an indication of past thinking of practitioners and academics on the subject.

Deininger (1977) argued that the informer performs a vital civic duty, although he concedes that there must be a reason for giving information. He lists six main reasons for being an informer. Payment, revenge, self-protection, damage to a competitor, secure esteem of the officer, and personal satisfaction.

O'Hara (1976) agreed with this list of categories, although he went further to suggest it was far from exhaustive, and depending on the circumstances of the particular relationship, there may well be other reasons involved.

Others have examined the motivational factors of informers. One was Katsampes (1971), who concluded that they could be separated into two main areas. Firstly, there are those who 'like the thrill of the skirmish' and in fact play the role of the police officer. Secondly, there are those who, having been arrested, are given the opportunity to help the police in exchange for a reduced charge or sentence, or even as an alternative to being charged. Such a practice is widely used throughout the world and accepted as legitimate incentive to recruit informers. A good example is in Hong Kong where officers of the Independent Agency Against Corruption (IAAC) tend to recruit all prisoners who are prepared to give information against their associates rather than serve long terms of imprisonment. Their situation is, however somewhat different to offenders in the UK, largely because UK officers are restricted by the Police and Criminal Evidence Act 1984 (PACE).

Dunnighan (1992) separates informers into categories, and he describes them as either 'regular' or 'supergrass'. He suggests that the reasons the latter inform is in order to receive a lighter sentence and, as such, their usefulness is short-lived. The regular, on the other hand, can go on providing information for a long time. We will see later though that this argument is flawed. Dunnighan assumes that an informer's motives do not change, whereas there is evidence to suggest that those who start informing in order to receive a reduced sentence continue to inform for other reasons.

Lee (1993) also supports the general consensus about informers motives and goes along with the accepted reasons of fear, revenge, money, repentance and altruism. However, he discusses what he calls the problem informer whom he describes as 'perversely motivated', who will offer services whether they be to identify undercover agents, learn police methods, identify targets and intelligence, or eliminate competition, as in drug sales. He suggests that this type of informer often infiltrates police departments to learn about traffickers, and supplies information about them as a decoy to divert police officers away from their own activities. It is interesting that the police service have recently begun to acknowledge Lee's portrayal, recognising the vulnerability of potentially corrupt officers who may be recruited to provide information to criminals thereby acting as an informer to them.

Reese (1980) discussed the characteristics of a psychopath whilst being handled by the police as an informer. He suggests that one reason why a psychopath may turn informer is that he may deflect the focus away from himself, and hopefully shift the investigation elsewhere. Reese conceded that such a person could be a successful informer, but any information he may give requires continual checking and corroboration. This type of person feels no guilt or remorse and cannot form a close relationship; they are untruthful, insincere and unreliable.

## A study of informers

In this chapter I want to examine the motivational factors of informers in England in more detail, and do so with reference to a more recent study where I looked at, amongst other things, the motivational factors associated with informing. This study sought to identify the reasons for informing, but also looked at how those motives may change over time, and the implications of such changes in terms of management issues for law enforcement agencies, and policy matters (Billingsley, 2000).

## Methods

As part of a larger study of informers throughout England (2000), 120 informers were asked for their observations and thoughts on their reasons for informing. Questionnaires were administered by way of semi-structured questions, with an open-ended format also being used to allow the respondents to provide answers in their own style. The aim of the questionnaire was to elicit as much information as possible regarding the relationship between the informer, his/her handler and the police officer. The motives which lead an informer to give information are important if this unique partnership between informer and handler is to be understood.

A total of 12 police forces and other law enforcement agencies throughout England agreed to participate in the study. In doing so they allowed access to sensitive material which, in the wrong hands, had the potential to corrode the integrity of the police service and damage the relationship between the informer and the police. It has to be said that a large number of other police forces refused access. Often, no explanation was offered, but some suggested that they were undergoing a process of self-examination as far as the use of informers was concerned. In the main, though, there was a reluctance by some forces to participate due to the sensitivity of the subject matter, and their fear that the findings might cause embarrassment or compromise them in some way.

It is recognised that most informers, but by no means all, have previous criminal convictions, or associate with criminals; this alone gives them the opportunity to provide the information needed by the police. However, by definition, their criminal background meant that their responses required a high degree of corroboration: indeed why should informers tell the truth to a researcher who in fact was a senior police officer, albeit from another police area? It was necessary, therefore, to put into place a number of tests and retests to check the validity of the responses. This was done to a certain extent by using the personal information provided by the informers which could be checked against existing police records.

Inevitably there had to be heavy reliance on the interviewer's experience and expertise in potentially misleading responses. In fact, the identifying impression from the interviews was that the informers were generally open and frank; the handlers on the other hand tended to be more evasive. Perhaps this was because they were reluctant to talk about their relationship with informers, especially to another police officer, in view of the importance they placed on confidentiality. On the other hand, it may have been that they were simply not willing to divulge information about their relationship because in doing so they would be obliged to admit breaches of the procedures.

## Motives of informers

The study examined why informers first became involved with the police. Table 5.1 sets out these findings, that is to say the main reasons informers gave for starting informing in the first place. Further reference in this chapter to motives, motivations and motivational factors in fact refer to the 'reasons' for being involved in informing, and these terms will be used interchangeably.

Table 5.1 shows the frequency distribution, in terms of the informers, reasons for starting as informers. It can be seen that there are a wide range of listed reasons although the top four account for 60 per cent (80 out of 120). The categories identified in this study largely support the findings of other research, that is the most common reason for starting is financial (32 out of 120). This was certainly uppermost in the mind of one informer who had this to say:

- 'If the money they're offering isn't enough, I won't bother. I do it for the money. I have something the coppers want – information. They have to pay otherwise they get nowt.'

One informer who was also involved simply for the money said,

- 'If you need money like I do, you have to come up with good information.'

Not all the respondents, however, were satisfied with the financial arrangements made on their behalf, for as one informer said,

- 'I was happy until recently. I got £55 million of paintings back and my share was £100,000, but I've been waiting for 2 years and I still haven't got it.'

**Table 5.1**   *Main reasons for starting to inform*

| Initial reason | Frequency |
| --- | --- |
| Financial | 32 |
| Dislikes that crime | 17 |
| Reduced sentence | 16 |
| Revenge | 15 |
| Right side of the law | 9 |
| Looking for a favour | 9 |
| Friendly with officer | 8 |
| Police pressure | 4 |
| Take out competition | 3 |
| Part of a deal | 2 |
| The challenge | 2 |
| Gratitude | 2 |
| Enjoyment | 1 |
| *Total number of reasons given* | 120 |

Inevitably, these financial matters also produce problems for the police. Over half of the informers in the study were unemployed, and probably claim unemployment benefit. They would also expect to receive money from public funds for their information to the police. The police service are under some pressure to examine this situation, and are looking at ways of ensuring that financial payments are subject to Inland Revenue scrutiny. There is no easy solution to this; the police service would rather not have to address this, knowing that it will raise important issues of disclosure and the protection of the informer's identity. Nevertheless, the police have an obligation to consider where they stand morally and ethically in this matter. This question is also relevant to the argument developed later about the way informers pass through a moral passage during their careers.

The second most frequent main reason for informing, as listed in the

Table above is rather more surprising; it is the informer's dislike for a particular type of crime (17 out of 120). One such informer was an ordinary, hard-working married man with no previous convictions. He had been an innocent victim of an unprovoked attack in a busy London street, when for no apparent reason a youth threw acid in his face, which resulted in substantial disfiguration. He decided to help the police in what he said was 'ridding the streets of violent crime so that decent people could go about their business in safety'. It appears that his fight against crime became an obsession.

One of the informers whose main reason for informing was financial, but also accepted that he enjoyed it said:

- 'I take satisfaction in taking the riff-raff off the streets, but I don't know if it makes any difference.'

Another informer who became involved as a result of his dislike of drug abuse explained:

- 'It's important to me. I want to wipe drug dealers off the face of the earth. It makes a difference to me, and the police need to know I'm genuine.'

Another added,

- 'I do it because crime is wrong. But there are devious reasons why some people inform. The police need to know if they're going to do a proper job.'

## Can the reasons change?

Law enforcement agencies generally recognise the need to understand the informers' motives, and most police forces advise their handlers to establish the informers' reasons for informing during the early stages of recruitment. It may be more important for police managers to establish whether those reasons change over the period the informer is giving information. Police forces have so far failed to acknowledge the significance of this. For example, if an informer gives information initially for financial reasons, but then at a later stage changes his reasons for continuing to do so, then it must be important for the handler to be aware of this change, if the relationship between them is to survive. The police handler can only properly supervise, manage and control an informer if he or she knows why the informer is giving information, not just at the beginning but throughout the whole of the relationship.

In this research the possibility of motivational change was examined.

The aim was to test the hypotheses that informers can change their reasons for informing, and to see whether they went through some kind of moral changes during their informing career. The results are shown in Tables 5.2 and 5.3. Table 5.2 shows how the initial reasons for informing change as the informing career progresses whilst Tables 5.3 shows the potential change of reasons over time.

In Table 5.2 the main categories shown in Table 5.1 have been collapsed into larger groups; the first group called 'own benefit' includes those informers who give information for some sort of reward or personal benefit to themselves, whereas those called 'social conscience and 'helping the police' include those who genuinely want to give assistance. The categories differentiate between the informer who wants to help himself and the informer who wants to help others. The results show that the majority of informers (86) are involved initially for personal benefit and the others (31) became involved through some genuine desire to help others, especially the police.

It is interesting that these categories largely correspond to Weber's definition of social behaviour; where he distinguishes between 'rational goal-oriented conduct', 'rational value-oriented conduct', 'affectual conduct', and 'traditionalist conduct – the last category being less relevant' as Weber considers this to have less practical value. 'Rational goal-oriented' behaviour' is utilitarian, having some meaning or objective, such as a reward; this largely corresponds to the first category. Next, 'value-oriented' behaviour is practised by someone who is 'guided solely by his convictions', for example someone who has high moral standards, and does what he does because it is right. This corresponds to those with 'a high moral conscience' who also 'help the police'. Thirdly, those operating according to 'affectual conduct' have 'emotional and passionate elements which may be determined where the action seeks revenge'. This type of conduct is about pleasing others through gratitude or merely taking some pleasure from a relationship; this also corresponds to that category concerned with helping others (Freund, 1968).

In Table 5.2 the category 'Own benefit' (86) includes those informers seeking financial rewards or a reduced sentence. It is the largest group and those informers within it rarely change their reasons for informing. The numbers in this category show a slight increase within the first two years. The next category those with a 'social conscience' (17), consists of those informers who are opposed to illegal activities such as drugs, and the numbers in this category also increase but after five years, i.e. amongst those who have been informing the longest.

'Helping the police' does not appear to be a great motivator at any period, and in fact decreases the longer the informer is active. Indeed this seems to be where the biggest change appears; there are substantially fewer informers who set out to help the police and who still wish to help

**Table 5.2** *Informers' reasons for informing – changes through time*

| Summary of reasons given | Initially | Within 1 yr | Within 2 yrs | Within 5 yrs | All informers |
|---|---|---|---|---|---|
| Own benefit | 86 | 86 | 89 | 85 | 83 |
| Social conscience | 17 | 17 | 17 | 20 | 24 |
| Helping police | 14 | 14 | 12 | 10 | 8 |
| Remove competition | 3 | 3 | 3 | 5 | 5 |
| Total number of reasons given | 120 | 120 | 120 | 120 | 120 |

them after five years, but these changes are slight. In any case, most of these informers still seem content to continue their activities so it may be that their initial motive of wishing to help the police has been sustained, with a few moving towards being more concerned to seek more personal benefit.

The numbers in the category of 'Removing competition' slightly increase as time passes, with a definite increase after the first two years of informing. The numbers are, however, small; even so, this may suggest that those in this group may not have achieved their goals, or perhaps they have identified new forms of competition. Whatever the explanation, these results must be of interest to the police, as there is a clear indication that 'taking out the competition' is for some a pervasive and important feature in the informer's life.

Generally speaking Table 5.2 seems to indicate that very little change occurs throughout the informer's career, at least in relation to the broad categories used. That is, those who start informing for personal benefit continue to do so throughout. There is a slight increase, however, in respect of those informers who begin out of 'social conscience' especially among those who want 'to help the police'. These groups account for the main changes. Overall, nearly half of the respondents in this category changed their reasons over time. Of course, those informers who said they wanted to 'help the police' may have been helping them in order to help themselves. Any information given to the police will be of help, but it is more likely that initially these informers seek some personal benefit, such as for example securing a reduced sentence.

It would appear from the data in Table 5.2 that there is little evidence to support the argument that most informers go through any significant moral change. However a more detailed examination is required if worthwhile conclusions are to be made.

In order to see how individual motives might change over time, an examination of the data was carried out looking at the reasons for starting, the propensity to change, and likely changes of motives. Table 5.3 shows the frequency distribution of the different reasons for starting informing (as shown in Table 5.1); the proportion of each group who change their reasons; what they change to; and at what point in time those changes are likely to take place. Here, we begin to see some real changes in individual motives.

Forty-two per cent of the informers changed their reason for informing at some time throughout their informing career, with 9 per cent of informers changing in the first year, 31 per cent changing within 2 years, and 39 per cent within 5 years. The percentage of informers who change seems to increase the longer they remain informers.

It is interesting to note that the only informers who change within the first year are those who started for 'revenge'. These informers changed

**Table 5.3**  *Breakdown of how reasons for informing are likely to change through time*

| Initial reason | Frequency | % who change | Within 1 year | Within 2 years | Within 5 years | At some time |
|---|---|---|---|---|---|---|
| Financial | 32 | 22 | | Enjoyment | Enjoyment | Enjoyment |
| Dislike that crime | 17 | 12 | | | Financial | |
| Reduced sentence | 16 | 62 | | Financial | Finan/Competition | Financial |
| Revenge | 15 | 93 | Financial | Finan/Enjoyment | Finan/Enjoyment | Dislikes that crime |
| Right side of the law | 9 | 22 | | Financial | | |
| Seeking favour | 9 | 78 | | Finan/Family | Finan/Dislikes crime | |
| Friend of officer | 8 | 25 | | | | Dislikes that crime |
| Police pressure | 4 | 100 | | | | |
| Take out competition | 3 | 0 | | | | |
| Part of a deal | 2 | 100 | | | Financial | |
| Financial | | | | | | |
| Challenge | 2 | 0 | | | | |
| Gratitude | 2 | 0 | | | | |
| Enjoyment | 1 | 0 | | | | |
| *Total* | 120 | 42 | 9 | 31 | 39 | 42 |

their motives to 'financial reward'. In fact, a high proportion of this category (93 per cent) apparently changed their motives at some time during their careers. Some informers started to enjoy their involvement, and where they continue for a long period they to begin to to dislike the types of crime they are informing about. So, if an informer no longer gives information as a form of revenge, then their objectives seem to have been satisfied; but rather than stop informing they may pass through a moral change, which begins with self-interest and leads to public interest.

It is suggested that those informers who started informing for financial reasons are unlikely to change (22 per cent), but if they do it will be because they start to enjoy informing. This result may be of interest to the police manager. Those who start because of so-called 'moral objections' or because they dislike a particular crime are very unlikely to change (12 per cent). One or two may eventually place a higher value on financial benefits, but by and large it is their moral objection which continues to dominate. In any case, they are not likely to change their reasons within the first two years. Clearly it would not be worthwhile for police managers to ask them to inform about things about which they do not have strong moral feelings.

It is interesting to note that a number of informers who started informing for different reasons actually began to dislike the crime about which they were informing. This includes informers who started for 'revenge', 'seeking favour', 'friend of the officer', or even those who started because they said they were under 'police pressure'. There is further support here, then, for the argument that informers can go through a moral change during their informing careers. Perhaps having learnt more about the implications of such crimes, through their association with the police, they begin to give greater support to the police objectives.

This was certainly the case with one informer who first became involved when he felt he had been badly treated by a fellow criminal. He decided to take revenge by giving information about this associate to the police, regarding his involvement in the trafficking of guns and weapons. After a while, the informer's knowledge about this particular category of crime increased, so much so that he became opposed to such activity. He continued to give information in order to help reduce the number of illegal weapons and stop those who were involved in it.

The study shows that those who start informing either to get a 'reduced sentence' as part of a deal, or for some other favour, are very likely to change, most probably after the first couple of years. The money will easily tempt them, so they are more of an easy target for the police. This is hardly surprising, especially regarding those who informed in order to get a 'reduced sentence'. Having achieved their goal, of course the motive will take them in another direction, but it is the new reason that will become important in the relationship between informer and handler.

A good example of this was an informer with an extensive criminal background. He had been arrested for burglary and was likely to go to prison for a long time. His only option was to provide information about his associates and other crimes, in order for the police to 'put in a good word' to the judge in his case. This resulted in a reduced sentence. He continued to give information during his term of imprisonment and on his release. His income from informing was sufficient to keep him away from committing crime, and although he was obliged to associate with criminals in order to provide useful information, he was able in time to earn an honest living. In this case at least, one criminal was diverted away from the criminal justice system.

It has already been noted that those who start informing for what has been called 'revenge' are extremely likely to change (93 per cent). They will often become attracted to the financial benefits, and in the medium term may even find they enjoy informing. In the longer term, they may develop a conscience and carry on informing out of a sense of public duty or because of moral considerations, but with so many changing one could speculate that their initial needs were satisfied. One such informer was a male with no previous convictions, whose daughter was a heroin addict. Out of pure 'revenge' against the drug trafficker who was supplying his daughter, he became an informer. Having become involved, he decided to continue his relationship with the police and informed for moral reasons, to try to help reduce drug abuse in his area. The data does not reveal how many other informers took this view, but clearly this was one example where an individual's morals could influence his motives.

'Revenge' itself could be closely allied with what has been called 'Taking out the competition', although the latter is less personal and may only occur when greed is an overriding factor. Table 5.3 clearly shows that those informers who originally wanted to 'take out competition' do not change their motives. The numbers in this category are admittedly small, but the informers in this category should nevertheless be regarded as a different type of individual to the informer who started for 'revenge'. It could be argued, then, that those informers who become involved for avaricious reasons will probably never change.

The minority who start informing for other reasons are not likely to change. These are people out of the mainstream, perhaps having fallen into informing through a friendship with an officer, while looking for a favour, or through gratitude for a favour done. Retaining these individuals will depend more on the continuation of that relationship than on the lure of other rewards, but if the relationship does break down, they may possibly be tempted to continue through financial reward. It would seem, though, that if this minority group do not begin informing for financial reasons in the early stages of their informing career, they are unlikely to do so later.

One issue which has not become apparent from the data, but which will clearly impact on the informer's motives, is the part the handler plays. Table 5.3 shows that financial motivation is not only the most common reason for an informer to become attracted to informing, but that if there is to be any motivational change it will probably be for those same reasons. However, it has been the practice for police handlers to give payment to an informer for information, even though that may not be their main motive for informing. This seems to have come about because the performance indicators used by the police have been linked to the amount of reward paid out to informers.

The use of informers is considered very important to police forces, particularly in relation to anti-drugs strategies, a point recognised by Newburn and Elliott (1998) who found that substantial effort had been put into producing performance indicators. It has been wrongly assumed that an increase in payments will reflect greater success in the use of informers. The police are required to show results and this may well have influenced the informer to change their reason for informing, and as a result, corrupt any moral change the informer may have been undergoing.

## Some tentative conclusions

An examination of informers' motives shows that the majority of informers start for financial reasons although there are many other diverse reasons why informers first become involved. These informers can be collapsed into two main categories:

- those informers who give information in return for some personal benefit

- those who do it as public-spirited citizens.

Further examination of the data shows that some informers change their motives during the time they provide information. Although few informers change within the first year, the numbers changing increase the longer they continue informing. So, for example, those informers who start for 'revenge' are likely to change their reasons within a year, and become more interested in financial rewards. Others however may never change, and remain the same throughout.

Some interesting conclusions can be drawn from this study. One is that the longer an informer continues to gives information, the more chance there is that they will change their motives. Indeed, very few will change within the first year, but those who do will have probably started for 'revenge'. These informers will change then for 'financial reasons', but then may begin to enjoy their relationship with the police handler. To speculate, it may be that an informer who sets out for revenge, and then changes his motives, has presumably achieved his original objective, that is to take revenge on an associate, witness or whatever. If this is so then it is surely crucial that the handler is aware of what is happening. This type of informer could be quite dangerous; the information he gives requires validating if that information is only given to satisfy feelings of revenge. There is always the possibility of being given false or malicious information, and more so when this is the reason.

The study has shown that those informers who started informing because they disliked a particular type of crime, are unlikely to change, at least within the first two years. This may include the illegal use of drugs. This raises an interesting issue in relation to the management of informers. Law enforcement agencies must ensure that the informers' motives are closely coupled with the type of information they want to obtain, if their work is to be successful. So, there would be little use in trying to secure information about unrelated crimes from an informer who only wants to give information about a specific crime, for example drugs. It follows then that police managers need to monitor and review regularly the motives of their informers.

This study provides some evidence to support the hypothesis that informers can pass through some form of moral change. As the relationship strengthens and progresses, some behavioural changes take place, which are bound to affect the relationship. The informer's purpose in continuing the relationship can take a different course, and this will clearly change their attitude towards their role and that of their partner.

There is evidence, too, that some informers who begin for personal benefit can become less mercenary and inform for more altruistic reasons. On the other hand, should an informer's motives change, whatever the initial reason, he is likely to find the financial potential far more attractive at some stage during his career.

## Implications for law enforcement agencies

The findings referred to in this chapter are clearly of importance to those who are responsible for creating policy in relation to the use and management of informers. It is suggested that it will no longer be sufficient to establish why an informer agrees to be recruited. The reasons for continuing must be reviewed and the longer they continue, the more important it is to review it. For example, with tight budgets and organisations which have become more accountable, managers are neglecting their duty if they allow informers simply to be financially rewarded, when in fact that was not their reason for informing. Moreover, if an informer gives information for reasons other than financial, it may be futile for controllers to tempt them with cash within their first year (unless the reason was for 'revenge' when, on the basis of the sample, the informer is quite probably going to be tempted by financial inducements). Similarly, law enforcement agencies must ensure that the performance indicators they use to provide management information is both meaningful and appropriate. The increase or otherwise of payments to informers does not in itself show how effective informers are; indeed, pressure on practitioners to show results could even alter the informer's motive for continuing to inform.

Finally, it must be recognised by managers that informers can indeed go through some moral change, and this will clearly affect the relationship that informers have with their handlers. That being the case, it is imperative that the relationship is continually reviewed to ensure that effective control is maintained, not just of the informer, but of the handler as well. Without a knowledge of motivational change, it is not possible to understand how that relationship develops and evolves. Law enforcement managers must accept that they have a duty of care to both the informer and handler.

# References

Association of Chief Police Officers (ACPO) (1995) 'National Guidelines on the use and management of informants and related issues'.

Association of Chief Police Officers and HM Customs and Excise (1999) *Public Statement on Standards in Covert Law Enforcement Techniques*, Use of Informants – code of practice, October 1999.

Billingsley, R. E. (2000) 'An examination of the relationship between informers and their handlers within the Police Service in England', unpublished Ph.D thesis, Loughborough University.

Brown, M.F. (1985) 'Criminal Informants: some observations on use, abuse and control', *Journal of Police Science and Administration* (USA) Vol. 13 no.3: 251–6.

Deininger, R. (1977) 'Using informants and co-operative witnesses', *Law and Order* (USA) July: 64–70.

Dunnighan, C. (1992) 'Reliable sources', *Police Review*, 14 August: 1496–7.

Ericson, R.V. (1993) *Making Crime: a study of detective work*. Second edition. Toronto: Toronto University Press.

Freund, J. (1968) *The Sociology of Max Weber*, London: Allen and Unwin.

Hanvey, P. (1995) *Identifying, recruiting and handling informants*, Police Research Group Special Interest Series: Paper 5, Home Office.

Home Office (1969) Circular No.97/1969, *Informants who take part in crime*.

Katsampes, P. L. (1971) 'Informants: motivations and inducements', *Police* (USA), Vol.16, December: 52–3.

Lee, G. D. 'Drug informants: motives, methods and management', *FBI Law enforcement bulletin* September: 10–15.

Newburn, T. and Elliott, J. (1998) 'Police Anti-Drugs Strategies: tackling drugs together three years on', Police Research Group Paper 89, Home Office.

O'Hara, C. E. (1976) *Fundamentals of criminal investigation*, Springfield, Illinois: Scott, Foresman & Co: 160–61.

Reese, J. T. (1980) 'Motivations of criminal informants', *FBI Law enforcement bulletin*, May: 23–7.

# 6 Gender issues in informer handling

## Teresa Nemitz

'... because women and men do not act separately in the social world, they are not independent of each other and their inter-relationship is a vital fact of life'.

(Smart, C., 1977 *Women, Crime and Criminology*: 179)

## Introduction

The inclusion of women in criminological writing and research has generally been neglected or a gender-neutral impression is conveyed. This is no less so in relation to police informants who are generally assumed to be men and handled by male officers. This chapter attempts to reinsert gender into the discussion about police informers by highlighting specific problems and issues about women informers, female police handlers and witness protection for women.

This chapter is based on data from questionnaires and interviews with twenty-eight female informers and interviews with female police handlers and staff in SO10 (a special operations department dealing with covert operations) of the Metropolitan Police. This data from the questionnaires formed part of a larger study conducted on police informers (the majority were men) which included the twenty-eight female informers discussed here (Billingsley, 2000). These women were registered police informers and lived in various parts of the country. In order to enhance the information gleaned from this research informal interviews were also conducted with a few female handlers in one police area. The information gained from the data, studies about female informers and interviews with female handlers raise some important issues that are relevant to the debate surrounding this 'dark' area of policing.

Just as the female offender commits all types of crimes for similar reasons as men, but fewer of them compared to men, so do women become police informers for the same reasons as men. Clearly, male and female registered police informers have committed offences; some commit offences while informing, but others, both male and female, have no criminal record and would not commit offences although they may have access to information about crime and criminals. Although some crimes such as shoplifting, fraud and forgery are often labelled as 'female crime', the question to be asked here is, does the same distinction hold for female informers? That is, what do female informers inform about – and why?

## Female informers

It is not known whether there is the same male–female ratio of offenders in the male–female police informer population. But the assumption is that the police informer is male. Although there are approximately 43,000 registered police informers in England and Wales there is no data which shows the male–female ratio (Billingsley, 2000). Consequently, the research that does exist about informers suffers from the same problems as many other criminological studies; although 'the informer' is often portrayed as gender neutral, there is the implicit assumption that the offender/informer is male and the handler is male. Therefore, we can reasonably assume that just as there are far fewer female offenders there are also far fewer police informers and fewer female handlers.

Why this should be so could be explained within the same theoretical explanations that are put forward to explain female offending. Or, as Heidensohn (1992) suggests, the reasons why there are fewer female offenders are similar to the reasons why there are fewer female judges, lawyers, police officers, etc (although the numbers of women in prison has risen faster than the male prison population in recent years (see Home Office, *Statistics on Women and the Criminal Justice System*, Section 95). The structural exploitation and/or oppression of women generally may well explain why there seem to be fewer female informers – or indeed, the reasons why there seem to be few female handlers. Of course, it could be argued that there is a link between the assumed low number of female handlers and the numbers of police women compared to men. According to Home Office statistics, in 1998 19,807 (16 per cent) out of 125,847 police officers were women. Out of the 28,175 officers on ordinary duty above the rank of Police Constable, 1,955 (7 per cent) were women. Out of the 151 Assistant Chief Constables, 8 were women and 2 of the 51 Chief Constable were women (Home Office, *Statistics on Women and the Criminal Justice System*, Section 95). However, there is no specific data about female detectives, their ages, length of service or other characteristics. Nevertheless, what we do know from the statistics is that there are more male police officers within all ranks; therefore it is reasonable to assume that the numbers of female handlers will also be small compared to male handlers.

## Characteristics of the female informers

One of the major issues that stand out from the data about these female informers is that their reasons for informing concern matters relating to their family or loved ones. That is, some women inform in order to keep a loved one out of trouble or, as one woman put it, 'just to keep an eye out for my family'. Other women have asked for, and been given, specific favours either for themselves or, as is usually the case, their family. For example, the handler of one woman, who had no previous convictions herself, said that her informing was to 'keep her family together'. This woman had agreed to 'set up a crime' in order to prevent her husband from becoming involved with criminal friend: 'some villains kept coming to my house and trying to involve my husband in jobs. I was able to plant drugs on one of them and then got him arrested when he left'. But this woman's handler could not resist inserting a contemptuous remark about this woman, and said, '[her] involvement is on behalf of her family. But she takes the money as well'. Several similar comments recorded by these women's handlers about them can only be construed as bordering on the contemptuous. This is interesting considering that the data reveals how highly these women regard their handlers; as one woman said, 'If my handler is happy I'll do what he says. He sorts everything out. I trust him, he wouldn't let me down.' It should be pointed out that these handlers are almost all male. Interestingly, no condescending remarks were recorded during the interviews with the female handlers.

The other reasons most often given for informing concerned their dislike of particular types of offending. Usually this meant drug dealing and in one case child pornography. Again, the women's dislike of drugs or drug dealers usually meant concern about a family member who was using drugs or probably involved in drug dealing, so that the police would 'not bother my sons'. Another woman gave her reasons for informing about drugs because, 'My daughter is on heroin, so I started doing all I can for the police to help.... It's important to me, I want to wipe drug dealers off the face of the earth. It makes a difference to me, and the police need to know I'm genuine.' This woman's handler asked her to 'set up a crime' by planting drugs in the house of someone she said was dealing in drugs. This woman's handler's comments again reveal contempt when he describes her as 'a petty thief who needs to think she is doing something for her heroin-addicted daughter, not very bright though'. However, this officer's view that she was 'not very bright' did not prevent him from using her as an informer, and she nevertheless seems to have helped this officer make arrests. Perhaps male handlers feel more secure with male informers whose motives they can relate to more easily, for example, money or 'taking out the competition' from other drug dealers.

All these women, except one, also informed for money, that is, they also received financial rewards as well as the favours. Clearly, earning money from informing was important as more than half the women were unemployed, only two were employed full time, seven women described themselves as having casual employment, and three said they were 'housewives'. Nevertheless, money was not the only factor, other concerns such as self-preservation, looking for a favour (for family and self) and friendship or gratitude were also important; friendship with the male handler also figured largely in their motivations for informing. Only one woman said her main reason for informing was to 'take out the competition'.

As mentioned above, one woman did not inform for money. She was described as being in her 20s and employed full time. Her motivations can only be described as moral and perhaps reckless. She stated that her reasons for informing were because, 'I want to stop crime hopefully. I am related to some not very nice people and I don't agree with what they do. I do it because crime is wrong.... The police need to know if they're going to do a proper job.' This woman had also agreed to give evidence in court, presumably against relatives. Her handler described her as 'a naïve young girl who is very vulnerable, honest and straight – but related to some very nasty people... she has given evidence in the box as an informer and is happy to do it'. In this case, although the handler views this woman with some respect, he also suspects that she might be in some danger but uses her, nevertheless, knowing that she is vulnerable. In a case such as this, surely there is a moral obligation on the part of the handler to ensure that their informer does not place herself in physical danger?

Clearly, the motivations or reasons for informing described by these women were more complex and sometimes confused that can be revealed in data gleaned from questionnaires. Some of the information contained in these questionnaires revealed events, motivations and reasons that portrayed a complex mixture of those mentioned above. For example, one woman described by her handler as 'an attractive blonde prostitute' kept a brothel, her motives for informing being a question of self-preservation, as the following shows: 'To look after myself I give info to the police. In my business I need them to be on my side, but it suits them as well. They wouldn't get the information if I didn't carry on business.' Yet this woman went to work as a prostitute for an escort agency in order to gain information about the owner who was dealing in child pornography. She did this because she didn't like child pornography, and for her handler – he could make a good arrest – and for herself, as she stated: 'In my brothel – he will help; for example one girl who works for me is on drugs. He has told me if the drug squad intends to bring out a warrant on her, he will tell me and make sure the place is clean.'

Two-thirds of these women were either divorced or single. Two-thirds had been informing for between two and five years and one woman for over six years. Most of the women had children, and altogether the women cared for 22 children between them; the divorced/single women had 16 children in their care. Also, two-thirds of the women admitted to having previous convictions. Nearly all their previous offences were for fraud or dishonesty, one was for drug offences and one was described as sexual.

When comparing the ages of the female informers with the male informers in the larger study (Billingsley, 2000), the males tended to be younger – in their early 20s to mid-30s – whereas the females were more evenly distributed across the age groups but were significantly over-represented in the 36-42 age group.

Further interesting observations are to be made when comparing the marital status of the informers. Thirteen (46 per cent) out of the 28 female informers said they were either divorced or separated. Only six females (23 per cent) said they were married compared with 42 males out of 92 (45 per cent). When comparing the 17 males and 18 females who were divorced or separated with the reasons they gave for informing, 14 out of the 17 males said they informed for personal gain. But the females' reasons were more complex and could perhaps be described as more altruistic or caring – particularly for their family members; but friendship, gratitude and financial reward were also part of the complex picture. The difference between the male and female informers' motivations is interesting. Although it would be reasonable to assume that the divorced or separated women might well be experiencing financial problems and informing for money, as far as these women are concerned that does not seem to be the case. Informing only for money does not convey the whole picture.

Moreover, when looking at the reasons given for informing by all the 28 female informers, again, only six could be described as falling within the definition of informing for personal gain. The variables available were described as 'reducing the sentence', 'looking for a favour', 'getting on the right side of the law', and 'taking out the competition'. However, looking more closely at the questionnaires, it appears that those who said their reason for informing was that they were 'looking for a favour', indicated that the favour was not always for themselves, or not for themselves alone. Favours usually involved helping or trying to protect members of their families. Other reasons given by these women for informing could be described as more altruistic, caring or traditionally feminine. For example, they were defined as: 'out of gratitude', dislike of the type of crimes they knew were being committed (these usually involved drug dealing and in one case child pornography). Two women said their 'friendship with the officer', that is their handler, was their main reason for informing. Over half of the females gave reasons for informing similar to those given by the male informers, that is, for personal gain in some way and/or financial reward. However, only 16 out of 102 male informers gave reasons for informing that could be described as altruistic. The proportion of women who did inform for selfless or altruistic reasons then takes on a different aspect. Indeed, it would be reasonable to assume that for many women who decide to become a police informer their reasons are far from materialistic, devious or spiteful.

Although it seems that some women's reasons for informing could be said to be altruistic, other reasons such as financial reward and favours were also important. But the relationship between these women and their handlers, even taking into account the scarcely veiled contempt of some handlers for their women informers, is fundamentally reciprocal – reciprocal in the sense that almost all of the women said they would not continue informing if they were not satisfied with what they got out of it. As one woman put it, 'If I needed some help on something and I didn't get it then I would lose interest'. Although a reciprocal relationship does exist between the informer and his or her handler, this does not mean that the relationship is equal – particularly in the case of women informers; however, neither could it be said that these women were being exploited by their handlers.

There is a strong case for undertaking further research on gender differences in police informers. The reasons why some women become police informants involves complex reasons, reasons that do not fall within the 'male standard' or expectations about the (usually male) police informer. Interestingly, the police occasionally appeal directly to women through the media asking for information. Such an appeal took place in March 2000 during a 'Crimewatch' television programme (BBC, 21 March 2000) when the police appealed directly to women to give information about the Stephen Lawrence murder. They appealed to wives, mothers or girlfriends and asked them to inform on their sons, husbands, boyfriends or ex-partners. The question is, were the police appealing to these particular women because they think they will inform on these men out of malice, deceit and/or money (although no financial reward was mentioned in this case)? Or are they appealing to a supposedly superior moral sense that they think women possess? However, if one takes into account the main reasons why the women in this study informed – mainly to keep their husbands or partners and sons out of trouble – it is doubtful if the police are using the right tactics in all such appeals for information. Unless another trial is brought about through information received from this appeal the public will not know if a woman has informed on her son, husband or ex-partner – and even then it is doubtful if the identity of the informer would be made known.

## Female police handlers

Information about female handlers in this chapter is gleaned from informal interviews with a small number of female police handlers. The total number of female police handlers is not known, but it is generally agreed that there are far fewer than men. Why this should be so is related to issues about lack of opportunity for policewomen. The statistics above show that only seven per cent of police officers above the rank of constable are women. Yet it is generally agreed by many male officers that women handlers are 'better at it' than men because they 'listen' and talk about female intuition.

Other reasons that may explain why there are apparently fewer female handlers concerns credibility: credibility about them as police officers and the credibility of the information they learn from their informers. Women officers know that they must perform better than male officers, and do so in order to be accepted as a credible police officer, particularly if they want promotion (Heidensohn, 1992). Consequently, policewomen feel that if they decide to use informers they take extra care to ensure that the information is credible. What this means is that not only should they as police officers have to be better than the men, but the informers they handle must be more trustworthy and more useful than the informers used by male handlers.

The female handlers agreed that the best informers, meaning those who give the most credible information, are members of the wider community, male and female, rather than the criminal world. They criticised the male handler's macho views about informers, the macho notion that informers have to be those giving information about armed robbery or busting the 'Mr Big' in the drug world. They criticised the male handler's image that informers have to be 'good criminals'. The female handler's relationship with their informers, particularly those ordinary people in the community, was based on mutual trust and respect. Interestingly, their 'community informers' were often recruited after they had complained to these policewomen about a problem; or the relationship had developed from being a witness or a victim of crime. What this means is that the relationship had formed because the complainant, witness or victim appreciated the way the female officer had dealt with their case. For example, a homosexual man who had been a victim of a homophobic attack did not expect much sympathy from the police and indeed did not expect the police to find the attackers. When the policewoman on the case treated him with respect and even charged the attackers, a valuable informer–handler relationship was then forged, based on mutual trust and respect. In this case, the information is given about problems within the homosexual community not for financial gain but because he trusts this police officer to use the information properly.

Another example of gaining a good 'community informer', this time in the Asian community, also came about through recognition that the female police officer treated the members of the Asian community with respect and sensitivity. So much so, that in this case the informer had 'recruited' a second generation into the relationship. Again, this is another example of good police work in the community, leading to the formation of a long-term informer/handler relationship. Of course most, but not all, of these 'community informers' also receive money, but their main reason for informing is that they trust and respect the policewoman.

These female officers also handled similar kinds of informers to those of their male colleagues, both male and female informers and often described as vindictive. But the vindictive informer is usually only useful once, and the female officers were convinced that the best informers were ordinary people in the community, and particularly the members of minority and ethnic groups. Interestingly, these female handlers talked about their police work generally and informer handling specifically in terms similar to that recorded by Frances Heidensohn about American policewomen (Heidensohn 1992). Heidensohn suggested that the American policewomen,

> preserved a notion of the moral possibilities of policing, and of women's role within that, notwithstanding what they had learnt about the *realpolitik* of everyday policing. The reasons for this are complex.... Common processes involve commitment to specific aims, especially to do with the community, to the causes of women and children and ethnic minorities, in other words to groups outside the police and often with low ranking in the police status hierarchy.

> (Heidensohn, 1992:134)

It seems that the way policewomen gain, use and treat their informers is in many ways different from that of their male colleagues. Their different approaches and degree of commitment reflect the way they, as policewomen, carry out their role generally. Further research is needed to determine the cost effectiveness of these somewhat different approaches – not only in relation to value for money, but also crime prevention and other issues that are not so easy to quantify, such as a community's satisfaction about justice.

## Witness protection for women

Some of the issues surrounding witness protection relating to women are discussed in this section.* Figure 6.1 shows the type or category of witness/informer who is allowed into the witness protection scheme. Once a witness and/or informant is accepted into the witness protection scheme their status changes – they are no longer informers. The types or category of witness/informer who are accepted into witness protection are complex. The definition of the resident informer is one who was an 'active

---

\* Acknowledgement is given to staff of SO10 of the Metropolitan Police and to others who cannot be named in the preparation of this section.

participant in a serious or series of crimes, who after arrest or conviction
elects to identify and give evidence against and provide intelligence about
fellow criminals involved in those or other offences' (Home Office, 1992).

**Figure 6.1** *Types of witness/informer in witness protection scheme*

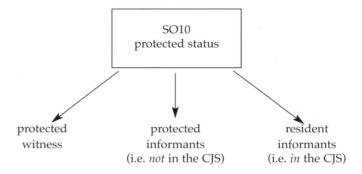

Resident informers are those in the criminal justice system – some may be
sentenced to prison, community service, or probation. But all have been
arrested and some may be convicted.

Participant informers (i.e. the protected informants) are not involved in
the criminal justice system. They may or may not have committed crime but
they inform about crime. The protected witness is someone not involved in
crime but has witnessed serious crime and is willing to give evidence.
Whatever their status, once admitted into the witness protection scheme they
are no longer active informers.

Although fewer women than men are admitted into the witness
protection scheme the number is rising and they pose particular problems.
Looking first at some of the reasons that draw women into witness
protection, one example would be a woman arrested for drug trafficking
who may decide to give Queen's Evidence in return for a reduced sentence.
If she goes to prison, protecting her is a problem because there are no secure
units for informers inside women's prisons. The options open to her may
include going on Rule 43,* or to brazen it out. Another option is for her to be
kept in a debriefing unit, which are available in some police stations in
London. The problem of children of course is a major issue for all women in
the prison system, but there are added implications for these women who
need security while in prison and may need to be relocated and change their
identity when released. There is no question that they could keep a baby with
them in prison; extended family or friends generally look after the children.

The security problem for these women reflects the lack of facilities

*Rule 43 – now rule 45 – whereby the prison governor can legally segregate a prisoner for
his/her own protection and/or for the interest of discipline in the prison.

generally for women in prison. Although we understand that the Prison Service are currently trying to address this particular issue, because of the smaller number of women needing secure protection, the Home Office have informed SO10 that it would not be cost effective to use scarce resource for this purpose.

Other reasons why more women are seeking witness protection is because the public generally are becoming aware that the police can offer witness protection, and for women particularly there is an awareness that the police are more willing to deal sympathetically with women victims of domestic violence and rape. Consequently, one of the main reasons why women are coming forward to give evidence against partners who are involved in serious crime is to protect themselves and possibly their children from physical abuse and rape. Most cases of domestic violence, rape, and race/hate crimes are dealt with at Divisional level by the Community Safety Units. However, there are an increasing number of women victims of violence who are so desperate to leave an abusive relationship that they are willing to give evidence about their partner's serious crime, even if giving such evidence would place their lives at risk and endanger their children. The witness protection scheme offers security, but it means being relocated to another part of the country or abroad. It also means new identities for the woman and her children. Further complications arise if these men demand to see their children. They have the right to see their children, but may use this right as a means of finding out where their mother lives. Although some men have applied to the court for access to their children it is very unlikely that leave will be granted once the judge understand the implications of witness protection.

Moreover, it is suggested that women particularly find being relocated, and undergoing a change of identify, more stressful than men. For women, relationships, particularly family relationships, perhaps matter more than they do for most men, and leaving extended family and friends is generally very hard to bear. The decision to go into witness protection is not taken lightly by these women, but essentially out of desperation.

Other reasons behind the increasing number of women seeking witness protection relate to the involvement of foreign nationals. These women may be the girlfriends of foreign national men who are involved in serious crime in this country – more often drug dealing, which usually includes violence. Their girlfriends may be willing to give evidence against these men and go into witness protection in return for resident status in this country. In these cases the Immigration Service must also be involved in the decision-making process. Clearly, the decision about whether a woman is accepted into a witness protection service like that currently organised by the Metropolitan Police is complex, and is doubly so if there are children. In view of the huge problem of domestic violence and the increase in international crime, particularly drug dealing, it is likely that the witness protection service may be used increasingly as a dumping-ground for women and children victims of violence.

## Conclusion

Many would see the qualities of the archetypal informer as belonging more to the female than the male. The traditional theories of female crime generally adopt one of two positions. One position perceives women who commit crimes as victims in a male-dominated society. The other portrays women offenders as being more cunning, crafty and devious than men, and able because of their traditional roles in society to hide their crimes (Pollak, 1950). There is another branch of early criminological theory which has long been discredited but nevertheless remains influential – biological determinism. The devious, neurotic, and 'evil' female criminal described in the early theories of biological determinism from Ferrero and Lombroso (1895) onwards continues to be depicted in literature, and portrayed in the media. Biological determinism attributes women's lower rate of criminal behaviour to their biological nature, which is passive and non-criminal, whereas criminality is more natural to men. Women who do engage in crime are therefore depicted as not really women, belonging more to the male sex. These classical theories of crime contain many prejudices and assumptions, such as the manipulative powers of women and the inherently deceitful nature of the female sex. Yet the questions remain, why are there not more female informers if women are more 'naturally' devious, deceitful, cunning and crafty than men, and why are there not more female police handlers if they are better at it than men?

The lack of research about informers generally and the numbers of registered female informers and female police handlers particularly, leaves these and many other questions unanswered. It is hoped that the gender issues raised in this chapter have highlighted some interesting differences about female informers and female handlers, and that identifying these may be valuable in determining future policy and practice. Moreover, the growing problem of women and children victims of violence seeking witness protection pose important questions which need to be acknowledged.

## References

Billingsley, R. E. (2000) 'An examination of the relationship between informers and their handlers within the Police Service in England', unpublished Ph.D thesis, Loughborough University.

Carlen, P. (1988) *Women, Crime and Poverty*, Milton Keynes: Open University Press.

Ferrero, W. and Lombroso, C. (1985) *The Female Offender,* London: Unwin.

Heidensohn, F. (1992) *Women in Control? The role of women in law enforcement,* Oxford: Clarendon Press.

Home Office (1992) *Resident Informers, Circular 9/92,* London: HMSO.

Home Office (1999) *Statistics on Women and the Criminal Justice System,* Section 95, London: HMSO.

Pollak O. (1950) *The Criminality of Women,* Philadelphia: University of Pennsylvania Press.

# 7 Juvenile informers

## Carole Ballardie and Paul Iganski

In view of the extent of crime committed by juveniles it would seem to be a logical step for police services to recruit juvenile informers. For some activities, teenage drugs dealing, gang violence, and criminal damage carried out by gangs of juveniles for instance, teenage informers may provide the only channel of intelligence. Yet the idea of using young people to inform on criminal activity has generated considerable controversy. On occasion the issue has been sensationalised by the news media in Britain. On one such occasion, in April 1995, the *Observer* newspaper revealed that 'Teenage "narks" may help cops'. The sensationalised language used by the press indicates the sensitivities involved. The *Observer* reported that, 'Police are considering setting up a network of teenage informers – some still at school – who could be paid by officers for providing intelligence on other teenagers' (Prestage, 1995). The *Daily Mail* reported that 'children could be recruited by police as school spies to help combat juvenile crime', suggesting that 'young informers could even be paid for tip-offs', and for telling 'crime tales out of school' (Halpin, 1995). A local newspaper, the Plymouth *Evening Herald*, reported to its readers that 'juvenile grasses' were being considered in a 'bid to beat criminals' (Grant, 1995).

The idea of using juvenile informers had the apparent backing of the then Home Secretary, Michael Howard. Other leading politicians supported the idea but raised questions about paying young informers. The MP Harry Greenaway, a former headmaster, believed that it was 'perfectly reasonable' for children to be used as informers. 'Very often they are the only ones who know', he said. But he warned: 'Payment can be a pressure to produce false witnesses and that is dangerous.' Similarly, Sir Ivan Lawrence, then Chairman of the Commons Home Affairs Select Committee, suggested that 'the only people likely to help put a stop to juvenile crime are other juveniles, but to pay them is another matter' (Prestage, 1995).

The potential for payment to induce the fabrication of evidence is not the only danger affecting the use of juvenile informers. There have been far more severe consequences. In 1998 a young informer used by the police investigating drugs dealing in Orange County, California, was murdered allegedly, according to his family, because it was discovered he was a 'narc' (Blair, 1998). Long before this murder, some of the limited academic literature on the use of juvenile informers had focused on the personal risks involved, particularly as a consequence of being 'found out' (Katz, 1979). Other commentators have focused on the legality of using juvenile informers (Herbert and Sinclair, 1977). The sensitivities, and the potential dangers involved, suggest that the use of juvenile informants by the police is not purely, or even mostly, an operational question of how the young informer should best be protected and managed. It is also not purely, or even mostly, a legal question. Instead, as we argue in this chapter, the question of juvenile informers is fundamentally an ethical question. It is about the types of citizenship values we wish to encourage young people to embrace.

## Action research on the use of juvenile informers

The flurry of media interest in Britain on the potential use of young informers by the police was sparked by a Home Office press release in 1995. It announced the successful projects that year benefiting from grants made by the Home Office Police Research Scheme. The project that aroused the media interest was an action research project that aimed to investigate the appropriate use and management of juvenile informers by the police service.*

When the research project was being conceived, the Association of Chief Police Officers (ACPO) National Guidelines on the Use and Management of Informants referred to the potential value of juvenile informers whilst advising that great care should be exercised when using them. But no operating instructions were provided by the guidelines other than those pertaining to adult informers. The achievement of a national standard in the management of juvenile informers provided a key objective for the research.

As there is little information about the use of juvenile informers by the police service in Britain, it is instructive to discuss some of the research project's findings. The project aimed to identify appropriate circumstances in which juvenile informers might be used, to determine appropriate ways

* The project was conceived and carried out by Sam Balsdon, a Detective Sergeant with the Devon and Cornwall Constabulary. One of the authors of this chapter, Paul Iganski, served as a consultant for the project, whilst working as a Senior Lecturer in Social Policy at the University of Plymouth. He advised on the research design, data analysis, and production of the final report. Thanks are due to Sam Balsdon, and the Home Office, for allowing the authors to draw extensively from the research for this chapter.

of recruiting them, and to provide some guidelines for the management of juvenile informers (Balsdon, 1996: 9). The research was carried out in a purposive sample of twelve police forces in England. The size of the sample was constrained by the resources available for the research in combination with an aim to achieve an in-depth qualitative understanding of the use and management of juvenile informers in the forces concerned. Forces were selected on the basis that they had either revised, or were in the process of reviewing their informant procedures; or alternatively that they had introduced innovative ideas in the management of informers. The aim was to learn from good practice.

A liaison officer nominated for the research in each force provided names of potential respondents selected because they were informer handlers. Semi-structured interviews were subsequently carried out in 1995 with 75 respondents. Most were from the CID or other plain clothes proactive units. Only two were women and therefore less than representative of the police service today. In an effort to encourage respondents to be frank about their experience of using juvenile informers the interviews were carried out under a guarantee of anonymity. The researcher did not reveal to anyone the names of respondents. A guarantee was also provided that the source of any revelations of unofficial, but lawful, practices would not be revealed.

The purposive selection of forces and individual respondents prevents any generalisation of the research findings across all forces. But this was not the intention of the research. The goal was to use insights from the experience of informer handlers to inform the design of guidelines for the use and management of juvenile informers.

## Protecting the welfare of juvenile informers

Transparent procedures for the use of juvenile informers provide a protection for the young person concerned, and also for the police officer handling them. The National Criminal Intelligence Service (NCIS) guidelines on the use of informants adopted in January 2000* specify that 'special care will be taken regarding the welfare and safety of juvenile informers' (para. 1.13.2). The safety of the young informer was also a concern for the informer handlers who participated in the action research project. Over half (39 of 75) believed that juveniles should not be used as informers in cases of serious crime as there is a particular risk of harm. As one respondent said, 'any drug traffickers you are investigating have violent tendencies. You'd have to be careful with juveniles because they're not like adults, they can't up and leave if it gets a bit hot. They can't move out of the area into a safe house.' (Balsdon, 1996: 21). Some respondents

* http://www.ncis.co.uk/web/Publications/use_of_informants_code3.htm

believed that juveniles shouldn't be asked to inform on their own parents, relatives and close friends. As one handler reported: 'I know his father was a known criminal and I'm not saying that I would ignore something that he told me, but I did not pump him about his father. I just let that one run.' (Balsdon, 1996: 22).

In view of the concern with the safety of the young informer, however, it was notable that out of the 62 handlers who were using juvenile informers at the time of interview, or who had done so in the past, a significant number (38) had not registered them. Their use of juvenile informers was therefore unauthorised.

Registration is part of a monitoring process that protects both the informer and the handler. ACPO guidelines on the use of informants at the time the research was being carried out stated that all informers must be registered. Operating instructions obtained from the forces in which the research was carried out also specified that all informers, whether rewarded or not, must be registered. By not registering juvenile informers the police officers concerned were not only risking disciplinary action if discovered, they were also undermining the integrity of the information they obtained. Courts accept the use of registered informers but rarely consider information provided by unregistered informers.

Respondent handlers provided a number of explanations for why they had not registered juvenile informers. Some (9) said that they were ignorant of any force guidelines for registration. More broadly, a substantial majority (82 per cent) of all respondent handlers participating in the research reported that they had no knowledge of any guidelines in their force for the use of juvenile informers. The lack of awareness was not just a matter of inadequate communication of guidelines by the forces involved. Nor was it simply a lack of diligence on the part of individual officers in failing to consult about appropriate procedures. Not all of the respondent forces had established instructions. This was despite the dissemination of the ACPO guidelines approximately six months before the research fieldwork was carried out. To supplement the interview material each of the twelve forces participating in the research were asked for their operating instructions for the use of informants. Three forces were unable to provide them, however, claiming that at the time of the research they were being revised to incorporate the ACPO guidelines. A further three forces made no mention of juvenile informers in their informant instructions (Balsdon, 1996: 21-22).

A substantial number of handlers who participated in the research (17) circumvented registration as they believed that procedural impediments would be created if they tried to register a juvenile. Some believed that it was the informal policy of their force not to use juvenile informers. As one officer stated: 'There is an unwritten force policy if you like – the impression that comes across is that it is discouraged to use juveniles'

(Balsdon, 1996: 17). There appeared to be some ambivalence about the use of juvenile informers in the forces participating in the research. One force was unambiguous, though, in its instructions. It explicitly prohibited the use of juvenile informers. Its instructions stated that persons under seventeen years of age must not be encouraged or cultivated to be informers, and that they would not be registered (Balsdon, 1996: 22).

The National Criminal Intelligence Service guidelines on the use of informants provide strong protection for juvenile informers. They are far more stringent than the requirements for adult informers. Whilst the guidelines are not legally binding, it was expected that all forces would comply with them within three months of their adoption by the NCIS in January 2000. The guidelines stipulate that within 72 hours of the provision of authorisation for the registration of a juvenile informer, the authorisation must be reviewed by a senior officer. In the case of the police and the National Crime Squad the review must be conducted by an Assistant Chief Constable, and by a Commander in the case of the Metropolitan Police and the City of London Police. Initial authorisation may be given for a maximum of one month after which time it may be renewed at intervals of not longer than a month, subject to the approval of the senior reviewing officer. The seniority of the officers involved in reviewing authorisation clearly reflects the concern with protecting the welfare of juvenile informers. The processes involved also indicate a recognition of the need to manage carefully police officers in the handling of juvenile informers and particularly to avoid the possibility of exploitation and malpractice.

The police role in the past with regard to welfare issues, however, has been an uneasy one. History indicates that although the police have had extensive involvement with such issues, much of this involvement has not been required by statute. Principles of welfare, justice and punishment have been entangled and confused in children and young offenders' legislation since the beginning of the last century. The Children Act 1908 established a separate juvenile court and the principle that young offenders would be dealt with separately from adults. Juvenile courts were empowered to deal with both the criminal offender and the non-offending but delinquent young person deemed to be suffering from neglect, or to have found themselves in bad habits, or bad company. In this way the troublesome and the destitute were conflated. By the time of the 1933 Children and Young Persons Act, offending delinquency and neglect had become synonymous, with the same form of state intervention prescribed for either.

The first police juvenile liaison schemes began in Liverpool in 1949, and gathered pace during the subsequent two decades. Initially controversial, these schemes gradually garnered acceptance, and section 5 of the Children and Young Persons Act 1969 sought to bring welfare and prosecution decisions together through statutory liaison between social services and police. Section 5 was never implemented, but in anticipation of this happening, juvenile bureaux were established to co-ordinate liaison between police and welfare agencies so as to enable a more informed decision to be made about prosecution, and these have lasted, despite section 5 being effectively repealed by the Criminal Justice Act 1991 (Thomas, 1994). Such initiatives as cautioning, diversion and intermediate treatment have developed under the auspices of juvenile bureaux, furthering police involvement in young people's welfare issues. As a separate enterprise, since 1958 the police have run Attendance Centres (Mair, 1997), and these too offer scope for a welfare role with young offenders.

The first direct mandate in law to the police regarding young people's welfare is laid down in Home Office Codes of Practice C and D for the Detention, Treatment and Questioning of Persons by the Police, issued in accordance with section 66 of the Police and Criminal Evidence Act 1984. But beyond requirements of procedure and physical care the police are expected to call in an appropriate adult to attend the young person in their custody. The Children Act 1989 and the Criminal Justice Act 1991 generated the legal separation between welfare and justice issues, with the removal of care proceedings from the criminal process and the establishment of the youth court and the family proceedings court. Since the early 1970s the police and social services have co-operated with other agencies concerned with child protection through the network of Area Child Protection Committees, though the police are not named by the Children Act (Thomas, 1994: 67).

We display an ambivalence about children and young people in our society. It is as though we cannot make up our minds about who or what a child is. Just as there is no absolute definition of when we attain adulthood, so there is no definitive indication of when childhood – or youth – begins or ends. This uncertainty is mirrored in our legislation. A child of 10 can be held responsible for a crime in England and Wales, a child of 8 in Scotland. A young person aged 16 may marry, but may not vote. Young people may seek full-time employment, but may not be eligible for unemployment benefits. They may buy a knife, but not a firework. They may buy tobacco, but not alcohol.

In the case of the criminal justice system, however, the ambiguity fades. There is a separate judicial system – the Youth Court, for defendants up to the age of 18 – and a separate custodial system. According to the Police and Criminal Evidence Act 1984, Code C on Detention, Treatment and Questioning, a juvenile (under 17 years old) should be accompanied by an 'appropriate adult', if detained as a suspect for questioning. Young people also have a separate non-custodial welfare system, recently redesigned according to the Crime and Disorder Act 1998 into multi-disciplinary

Youth Offending Teams, including social workers, police officers, probation officers, education welfare workers, and health workers.

As the primary law enforcement agency, contemporary police services are the first port of call when young offenders come to the attention of the public, yet their welfare role has been limited to procedural matters and notification and involvement of other agencies. Although the Police and Criminal Evidence Act 1984 allots them a welfare responsibility, they are then required to call someone else in in order to fulfil that responsibility. However, along with all criminal justice agencies, the police in Britain have lately been the subject of 'joined-up' thinking. With the advent of the Crime and Disorder Act 1998 they find themselves actively involved with the welfare of young offenders by virtue of their secondment to the Youth Offending teams. This is a logical progression from the inter-agency involvement developed through diversion and cautioning schemes in the 1980s and 1990s, with the police involvement now clearly specified in law (Brayne and Martin 1999).

Youth Offending teams follow the example of their predecessors, Youth Justice teams, in that they remain under the auspices of local authority social services departments, and thus retain the legal mandate of children's legislation. The Youth Court has a statutory duty mandated by The Children and Young Persons Act 1933, section 44(1), endorsed within section 17 of the Children Act 1989:

> every court in dealing with a child or young person who is brought before it either as an offender or otherwise, shall have regard to the welfare of the child or young person and shall in proper cases take steps for removing him from undesirable surroundings and for securing that proper provision is made for his education and training.

Thus evaluation of the police use of juvenile informers occurs at a pivotal time for the police. A political context that demands toughness on crime, and on youth crime in particular, requires that the police respond to political and popular demands to manage, prevent and reduce youth crime as best they can. At the same time, under the auspices of the Crime and Disorder Act and the United Nations Convention Treaty on the Rights of the Child (UNCRC), the police are officially given duties in respect of child protection obligations. If police work with juvenile informers is to observe existing child protection law and the UNCRC then it demands a protocol that would operate within these confines.

This arguably necessitates the extension of decisions about the appropriate use of juvenile informers and the subsequent monitoring of their use beyond police services alone. As informers are commonly involved in criminal activity, or on the margins of criminality, a strong argument can be made that there is a duty upon the police to inform parents of their child's activities. It may be the case that the child's parents themselves are involved in criminal activity. The NCIS guidelines stipulate that the use of a juvenile to provide information about members of their own immediate family will be 'exceptional' and 'requires the most careful consideration of the question of proportionality' (para. 4.2). More generally, the guidelines specify that where a parent or guardian has not been advised of the child's activities as an informer, records will kept about the decision to take this course of action (para. 4.7). Whether or not the parents have been informed the relevant child protection agency – the Local Authority Social Services Department – should be informed of the young person's involvement. They should especially be involved if any child protection decisions are indicated. The multi-agency co-operation established under the Crime and Disorder Act 1998 might facilitate the necessary communications.

## Promoting good citizenship

Childhood and adolescence is a period of transition. While traditional theories of human development may vary in many respects, they are united in the view that adolescence is a stressful time in terms of role transition and role conflict. While it is important to acknowledge that this transition is relatively untroubled for the majority of young people, for a minority it is a period of stress and uncertainty. Moreover it is a transition which has lengthened in recent years, as a combination of reduced employment opportunities and changes in benefits legislation has reduced the likelihood of young people achieving economic independence, and the consequent freedom and responsibilities that once accompanied moves toward adulthood. Adolescence is a crucial time for the development of identity, and whereas at one time young people followed clearly demarcated routes through school and the labour market, as their parents had done before them, since the 1980s the points of reference are no longer clear (Furlong and Cartmel, 1998). An uncertain and changing world indicates threat and risk; the old role models no longer apply. Within this turmoil, guided only by a welter of changing social and cultural influences, young people must try and establish an identity that holds meaning for them and fits into their social world.

Attitudes toward young people have also changed. There was arguably once a concern with young offenders' welfare, but today there is more of a concern with punishment and containment. The 1990s were characterised through our television screens and newspaper headlines by images of wayward demonic youth, perpetuating a torrent of lawlessness, violence and brutality. The hue and cry evoked by the media was followed by a welter of experimental and legislative measures designed to contain and combat youth crime, most recently the Crime and Disorder Act 1998

(Muncie, 1999: 6-7). The legacy of fear of youth crime endures. Within this context it is easy to forget that uncertainty and insecurity endures in young peoples' worlds. Young people who attract the attention of law enforcement authorities are likely to be badly behaved, truculent, full of bravado. They may have adopted lifestyle activities inappropriate for their age. It is easy to forget how young they really are.

In considering the ethical implications of police practice with juvenile informers, it is necessary to acknowledge that young people need adults, and must depend upon them for support and guidance (Noller and Callan, 1991). Beyond their families, young people have high expectations of the adults they encounter. They hope for, and expect to receive, support, encouragement and affirmation of themselves and their aspirations. When they come into contact with adults they hope to be treated with respect and listened to (Catan *et al*, 1996). But young people are also vulnerable. They have no political power. They cannot vote, and they generally have relatively little social or economic power. Diminution of the rights of citizenship afforded to young people, through erosion of their rights to state benefits, poor employment opportunities and poor housing opportunities, has led to their increased poverty and inequality, and an increased reliance upon decisions and actions by adults in positions of power to enable changes in their lives.

Young people are arguably impressionable, and easily influenced. Those who find their way, for whatever reason, into the criminal justice system, are perhaps among those most in need of the citizenship training proposed by the Labour government elected in 1997 (Blunkett, 1998). The law, the criminal justice system, and the police as representatives of that system inform and shape young people's views of our society as future citizens. It is, therefore, arguably incumbent upon the police to be examples of moral, measured, fair and just behaviour in their contribution to that process (Furnham and Stacey 1991: 160). We would further suggest that the police, along with all other public sector agencies concerned with young people, have a responsibility to set a good example in the way they behave as individuals – to offer a pro-social model of good citizenship. The practice of pro-social modelling by staff involved in rehabilitation programmes is endorsed by the Home Office.

> Probationers are motivated by the probation officers' legitimate moral authority.... The method known as pro-social modelling is linked to the concept of legitimacy. This entails being clear of (sic) one's values and objectives and reinforcing them with offenders through praise, reward and sanction
>
> (Chapman and Hough, 1998: 58)

Pro-social modelling has a specific focus. It is about people who work with offenders being clear about their role as a positive example to offenders, whilst not reinforcing any pro-criminal thoughts and behaviours to which offenders are prone (Gast and Taylor, 1998: 3). In adopting an approach like this police officers might be legitimated as upholding values of inclusion and citizenship toward the young people they deal with.

It is highly questionable, however, whether the encouragement of young people to act as informers and to reward them financially for the information they supply, provides an appropriate message about citizenship. The issue of whether, or how, young people should be paid or remunerated financially or otherwise, was one that raised perhaps the most concern and discomfort amongst informant handlers who participated in the action research project. They were asked whether they believed there were any ethical problems in rewarding juvenile informers. Some were concerned that the anonymity of informers would be compromised by cash payments. One handler stated: 'I think you have got to be very wary about handing them money as to what they're going to do with it and how they are going to spend it, and how they are going to explain it to their parents.' In contrast, another respondent believed that: 'The sort of person I deal with is not likely to have problems in explaining where he got the money from. The fifteen year-olds in the streets of... could say they got money from crime and they would be believed.' (Balsdon, 1996: 18). Some handlers were concerned about what cash rewards might be spent on. As one respondent reported, 'The last thing we want is giving these kids £100 to blow it all on drugs or whatever.' Various alternatives to rewards involving a cash payment were consequently suggested by respondents.

Payment for information, however, whether in cash or by another means, is perhaps the component from the practice of handling adult informers that translates least easily into the handling of young people. The issue is not simply an operational problem of protecting the anonymity of informers or controlling what they might spend the money on. The possibility of financial remuneration or payment in kind raises the possibility for manipulation, misinformation and corruption on either side, or between parties. It may encourage young people to become involved in criminal activity for the rewards they gain for information. Police services may therefore potentially contribute to the delinquency of the young people concerned. Beyond these potential dangers, there is a further fundamental consideration. Payment for information is arguably a practice that cannot be sustained within a model that seeks to engender and nurture a concept of good citizenship within young people. The establishment of a cash nexus for information about criminal activity arguably sends a message to young people in their formative years that co-operation between police services and the citizens they serve is based upon a relationship of mutual self-interest, an exchange of cash for information. Arguably, this is not a desirable model of civic participation to promote amongst young people. The objection is not about young people voluntarily providing information to the police, it is about the conditions under which the information is provided.

In mitigation of police practices in recruiting juvenile informers, the young people concerned are generally involved in the criminal justice process prior to recruitment, and therefore connected to circles involved in offending. The action research project with informer handlers hardly revealed the establishment of networks of teenage informers in schools as suggested by some of the press reporting. As is common with informant recruitment in general, the respondents had recruited their juvenile informers after dealing with them as prisoners. The NCIS guidelines on the use of informants observe that 'Such and individual will typically have a criminal history, habits, or associates…' (para. 1.14.1). Hence the decision as to what appropriate use may be made of a juvenile informer is arguably dependent upon the circumstances in which the young informer is recruited (Herbert and Sinclair, 1977: 190–91). Yet even those young people involved in, or associated with, criminal activity have rights and responsibilities of citizenship. In effect, young people are 'apprentice citizens' (Storrie 1997: 65) and their citizenship skills are to be learned. All young people have the potential to become criminals, but they are all also future citizens. Young people develop a sense of right and wrong, and behaviour which reflects that sense of understanding, from the adults around them and how they are treated by those adults.

There is a danger of seeing young people who come to the attention of law enforcement agencies only as potential criminals, and not as young people in possible need and distress and at a formative stage in their development. There is a danger effectively of seeing them as 'damaged goods'; this must be resisted. As Alun Michael – a former Home Office Minister – has argued:

> Young people should be involved in the search for solutions to youth crime rather than ignored as though they are part of the problem we need to get young people talking about citizenship and the consequences of crime in a way that is meaningful to them. We must help them to think for themselves so that they can make informed choices about their own actions and reject anti-social behaviour.
>
> (Michael, 1998)

In this context, whilst stringent procedures may be established to protect the physical welfare of juvenile informers they cannot protect their moral welfare.

# References

Balsdon, S. (1996) *Improving the Management of Juvenile Informants,* London: Home Office Police Research Group.

Blair, J. (1998) 'Ethics of using juvenile informants', *Christian Science Monitor,* 14 April.

Blunkett, D. (1998) 'New report points the way to citizenship education for all pupils', U.K. Department for Education and Employment, Press Release, 22 September.

Brayne, H. and Martin, G. (1999) *Law for Social Workers,* Oxford: Blackwell.

Catan, L., Coleman, J. and Dennison, C. (1996) *Getting Through: Effective communication in adolescence,* Research Project Funded by the BT Forum, Brighton: Trust for the Study of Adolescence.

Chapman, T. and Hough, M. (1998) on behalf of HM Inspectorate of Probation, *Evidence Based Practice: a guide to effective practice,* London: Home Office.

Furlong, A. and Cartmel, F. (1997) *Young People and Social Change: Individualisation and risk in late modernity,* Milton Keynes: Open University Press.

Furnham, A. and Stacey, B. (1991) *Young People's Understanding of Society,* London: Routledge.

Gast, L. and Taylor, P. (1998) *Pro-social Modelling Handbook,* Midlands Probation Training Consortium and Shropshire Probation Service.

Grant, S. (1995) 'Juvenile grasses considered in a detective's bid to beat criminals', *Plymouth Evening Herald,* 25 April.

Halpin, T. (1995) 'Police could pay cash for crime tales out of school', *Daily Mail,* 24 April.

Herbert, D. and Sinclair, L. (1977) 'The use of minors as undercover agents or informants: some legal problems', *Journal of Police Science and Administration,* 5(2): 185–192.

Katz, H.A. (1979) 'Use of juveniles as police informants', *Journal of California Law Enforcement,* 4: 196–198.

Mair, G. (1997) 'Community Penalties and the Probation Service', in Maguire, M., Morgan, R. and Reiner, R. (eds) *The Oxford Handbook of Criminology,* Oxford: Oxford University Press.

Michael, A. (1998) 'Youth Crime: we must involve young people in the solution', U.K. Home Office, Press Release, 16 March.

Muncie, J. (1999) *Youth and Crime: a critical introduction,* London: Sage.

Noller, P. and Callan, V. (1991) *The Adolescent in the Family,* London: Routledge.

Prestage, M. (1995) 'Teenage "narks" may help cops', *Observer,* 23 April.

Storrie, T. (1997) 'Citizens or what?', in Roche, J. and Tucker, S. (eds) *Youth in Society,* Milton Keynes: Open University Press.

Thomas, T. (1994) *The Police and Social Workers,* Arena.

# 8 Where the grass is greener?
## supergrasses in comparative perspective

### Steven Greer

## Introduction

Derived from the Cockney rhyming slang 'grass' for informer,[1] the term 'supergrass' was first coined by journalists to refer to the London gangsters who 'turned Queen's evidence' in the early 1970s. It was then applied, at various points in the next three decades, to the ex-terrorists who did likewise in Northern Ireland, in Italy and in Germany, and to cooperative *mafiosi* both in the US and in Italy (Greer, 1995). While a supergrass may merely be a police informer who supplies information on a grand scale, those in question provided a crucial extra contribution: giving evidence for the prosecution in open court in a series of typically mass trials. Why did they appear in such numbers, and when and where did they do so? What light do these experiences shed on perennial questions about effective and legitimate law enforcement in liberal democracy? In seeking answers to these questions the domestic experience can be compared and contrasted with its overseas parallels in a variety of ways. But a central distinction concerns the kind of offences against which the supergrasses were targeted: organised crime and political violence.

## Organised crime

### The supergrass process in England

Although by no means the first trial on informer evidence in the history of English criminal justice (Radzinowicz, 1956), the modern English supergrass process was a direct response to a dramatic rise in the incidence of serious organised crime in the early 1970s – particularly bank robberies in the London area – and an official perception that existing methods of dealing with it were ineffective (Criminal Law Revision Committee, 1972: para. 21; Mark, 1972: 6, 13). It began on 23 December 1972, when Bertie Creighton Smalls, a key member of a network of bank robbing gangs then under arrest, offered to name all his accomplices in exchange for his freedom. A deal, centring upon a written guarantee of immunity from prosecution, was struck with the DPP. No evidence was tendered against Smalls when he appeared in court on 13 July 1973 accused of a catalogue of serious offences. Having been released he subsequently appeared as the key prosecution witness in three trials involving 25 defendants, 16 of whom were ultimately convicted.

Deciding the appeals in the Smalls case the Court of Appeal both endorsed the practice of prosecuting large numbers of defendants upon the testimony of a supergrass and indicated the appropriate parameters (*R. v Turner* 1975). These were as follows. First, trials should be less complex. Secondly, the Director of Public Prosecutions should not grant such wide immunities in writing. Thirdly, convictions should not be obtained without the supergrass testimony being corroborated or supported by other evidence. Offers of immunity were, therefore, abandoned in favour of prosecuting potential supergrasses prior to them testifying as key Crown witnesses (Seymour, 1982). However, the DPP did not issue instructions that there should be no further prosecutions on the uncorroborated evidence of supergrasses until the day the appeals in the case of the second supergrass, Maurice O'Mahoney, were heard (*The Guardian*, 19 May 1977).

Even before all the trials in which Smalls gave evidence had been completed, the next two supergrasses, Maurice O'Mahoney and Billy Williams, were in custody. O'Mahoney was arrested on 12 June 1974 and appeared in court three months later admitting to 102 offences including 13 armed robberies and 65 burglaries. The only witnesses were two police officers who assured the court that he had provided even more information than had Smalls. Accepting the value of O'Mahoney's co-operation, the judge sentenced him to five years' imprisonment, although on the basis of his record he could have expected at least 15. Between the summers of 1975 and 1976 O'Mahoney appeared as a prosecution witness in a series of trials, and in the spring of 1977 he was called by the Crown to support the evidence of Billy Williams. The appeals in the biggest of these cases, involving 13 appellants, were heard by the Court of Appeal in 1977 and provided a second opportunity for some judicial influence to be exerted upon the use of supergrass evidence (*R. v Thorne* 1978).

The Court of Appeal's decision followed that in the Smalls case by endorsing the use of supergrasses as a method of prosecution, but the size of the trials was criticised, and once more the need for corroborative and supportive evidence was emphasised. On 15 March 1976, a mere 21 months after he was arrested, O'Mahoney was released on parole. Apart from a few months, all his time in custody had been spent in a police cell. He subsequently failed to appear at the trial of the remaining accused, who were set free with verdicts of not guilty entered on their records (O'Mahoney, 1978: 211). The negotiations between courts and prosecuting authorities represented by the Smalls and O'Mahoney trials, and the subsequent alterations in prosecution policy, established a *modus vivendi* which allowed a succession of supergrass cases to be processed comparatively smoothly.[2] Lenient sentences replaced immunity from prosecution as the main reward for co-operation with discounts of from a half to two-thirds depending on the circumstances and the assistance the police attested the supergrass had provided (see *R. v Lowe* 1979; *R. v King* 1985; *R. v Davies and Gorman* 1978; *R. v Tremarco* 1979; *R. v Rose and Sapiano* 1980; *R. v Sinfield* 1981; *R. v Preston* 1978). The Home Office reduced the level of punishment further. As a result of the exercise of the Crown prerogative of mercy it seems that no English supergrass at this time served more than two years of his sentence (Seymour, 1982).

Seymour maintains that comparatively few of the scores of people arrested on supergrass evidence in the 1970s were eventually convicted, and that, although there was a definite drop in the number of serious robberies in the London area following the conviction of the Smalls gang, from the mid-1970s to the early 1980s the annual number of serious crimes almost trebled while the number of supergrasses multiplied (Seymour, 1982). According to Campbell, the English supergrass process declined from the late-1970s onwards as the focus of organised crime shifted from armed robbery to drugs and as doubts about the reliability of supergrass evidence increased (Campbell, 1994: 160–3, 1991; Morton, 1995). By the 1990s such trials were rare.[3] Unlike the loose structure of the gangs hand-picked for particular armed robberies, the close-knit and stable networks of drugs suppliers proved more difficult for informers to penetrate. With greatly increased stakes, the underworld also became much more willing and able to punish betrayal with murder or mutilation. Several supergrasses re-offended and admitted having given perjured evidence at the trials in which they had been the principal Crown witnesses. Still others withdrew their co-operation once they reached the courtroom having wasted large sums of public money in the process. It was not surprising, therefore, that juries became increasingly sceptical of their evidence.

## The US Witness Protection Program

The US has not seen a supergrass process in quite the same sense as England, Northern Ireland, or Italy, although mass trials on the evidence of mafia informers have taken place (Greer, 1995: 223-33). The US parallel has instead been characterised by a formal system of protection offered to vulnerable witnesses including, but not limited, to those involved in organised crime, a reluctance to prosecute large numbers of defendants in single trials, the provision of other evidence (particularly that obtained by surveillance) to corroborate informer testimony, and continued reliance upon the tradition of jury trial to gain convictions in spite of obvious risks to jurors.

Following the 1967 US Task Force on Organised Crime, which identified inadequate protection for vulnerable witnesses as a major law enforcement shortcoming in this context, title V of the Organised Crime Control Act 1970 established the Witness Protection Program. Amongst other things, this authorised the Attorney-General to provide short-term or permanent protection plus new identities, credit cards, indefinite subsistence payments, fictitious work histories, military service records and school reports, to vulnerable witnesses involved in organised crime trials – the majority of whom are offenders – and to their families. In 1984 the Witness Security Reform Act repealed this legislation and overhauled the process in order to offer the public greater protection against recidivism by protected witnesses themselves (Levin, 1985; Lawson, 1992).

By the end of the 1990s commentators reported that the Witness Protection Program, allied with powerful social factors, had hit the US-Italian mafia hard (*The Guardian*, 19 May 1998). The pursuit of self-interest had undermined traditional codes of loyalty, honour, and most of all, silence (the so-called 'Americanisation' effect) and had led to an unprecedented number of *mafiosi* informing on each other. Between 1980 and 1985 2,254 mobsters were indicted in 1,025 trials in New York, Chicago, Boston and elsewhere (*The Guardian*, 30 December 1987) and between 1 October 1981 and 31 December 1986 the FBI reported that over 850 Cosa Nostra members and their associates had been convicted (Organised Crime Section, US Department of Justice in Centro Nazionale di Prevenzione e Difesa Sociale, 1987). Up to 1986 some 10,000 'very serious criminals' had been found guilty in trials involving protected Federal witnesses and the sentences they received were, on average, twice as long as those in similar cases in which protected witnesses had not taken part (*ibid*). In 1985 'Fat Tony' Salerno and four other elderly members of the 'Commission' – a consortium of organised crime bosses described as the US mafia's 'Supreme Council' – received sentences of 40-100 years for racketeering, and in 1987 the $1.6 billion 'Pizza Connection' case resulted in a further 18 convictions for the distribution of heroin through a chain of fast food outlets (*The Guardian*, 30 December 1987; Blumenthal, 1989; Alexander, 1989). In both trials the testimony of supergrasses Tommaso Buscetta and Savatore Contorno proved critical to the prosecution (Shawcross and Young, 1988: 26). On 2 April 1992 John, the 'Dapper Don', Gotti (reputedly the last of the mafia heads of families then still at large) was convicted in a trial which hinged on the testimony of his underboss, protected witness Salvatore ('Sammy the Bull') Gravano, who was also responsible for 'the conviction, guilty pleas or extended prison terms of dozens of Cosa Nostra key figures' (Maas, 1987: 297, *The Guardian*, 3 April 1992). By the end of the decade, in New York alone, 14 senior *mafiosi* had reputedly turned states evidence and up to 100 were said to have been taken on to the Witness Protection Program (*The Guardian*, 19 May 1998).

## The Italian anti-mafia *pentiti* process

The Italian anti-mafia *pentiti* ('repentants') trials have been on an awesome scale with single cases often involving hundreds of defendants (Greer, 1995: 239–42). Following similar and highly successful proceedings against the Red Brigades (see below) they began, in the organised crime context, with the arrest in the United States in 1984 of Tommaso Buscetta – the most celebrated supergrass of modern times – who claimed that his decision to collaborate with law enforcers stemmed from the mafia's departure from its traditional code of honour. Buscetta's information, plus that of Salvatore Contorno, led to the first 'maxi-trial' involving 475 defendants in the specially constructed 'bunker' courtroom inside Palermo's ancient Ucciardone prison. In December 1987, 22 months after it had begun, the trial's 350th session ended with 338 convictions (*Independent*, 16 December 1987).

But the *'pentiti* process' which followed was dogged by controversy and marked by peaks and troughs. In the 1980s hundreds of other defendants were convicted in a string of trials, involving both major and minor supergrasses, as disaffected and frightened *mafiosi* broke the traditional code of *omertà* (silence) and turned states evidence in order to evade, and wreak personal vengeance upon, their increasingly dictatorial and violent leaders (*The Guardian*, 30 October 1997). But in February 1989, 80 allegedly prominent *mafiosi* were acquitted in Palermo's third bunker trial when the testimonies of *pentiti* were rejected. By early 1989 only 60 of those convicted in the original maxi-trial were still in prison (*The Guardian*, 9 June 1995) and a formal witness protection scheme was not established until 1991 (Falcone with Padovani, 1992: xvi, 46). In the summer of 1992 the mafia war entered a further deadly phase with the murder of Italy's two most experienced anti-mafia investigating magistrates, Giovanni Falcone and Paolo Borsilino, amidst suspicions that they had been betrayed by pro-mafia elements within the state itself.

The authorities responded with uncharacteristic determination to the challenge which these high-profile killings represented. In June that year legislation was passed which formalised the contribution of *pentiti* and guaranteed reduced sentences and protection (*The Guardian*, 10 and 13 July 1992). A spate of arrests followed, including that of Salvatore Riina, the alleged godfather of the ruthless Corleonese clan, whose 'dishonourable' activities Buscetta claimed had prompted him to turn state's evidence in the first place (*The Guardian*, 15 April 1993). Riina's trial, which involved over 40 accused, began in the spring of 1995, featured the evidence of some 50 *pentiti*, and ended on 26 September 1997 with the conviction of all the principal defendants for, amongst other things, the murder of Falcone, his wife and their three police bodyguards (*The Guardian*, 27 September 1997). The number of *pentiti* rose throughout the 1990s and, by 1996, over 420 had taken advantage of the 1991 law (*The Guardian*, 30 October 1997). But by the middle of the decade the anti-mafia campaign had lost momentum. Concerns about the reliability of *pentiti* evidence led to tighter controls on its use and several key convictions were overturned on appeal (Greer, 1995: 241). Doubts also surfaced about the motives of some 'repentants', including Contorno, who were alleged to have collaborated with the authorities to eliminate rivals in order to facilitate their own return to crime (*The Guardian*, 30 October 1997). The will to tackle the mafia also faltered as Italy succumbed to a series of familiar political crises (Stille, 1995).

Although over 1000 *pentiti* were on the witness protection programme by the end of the decade its credibility was seriously damaged in September 1999 when former prime minister Giulio Andreotti was acquitted of mafia-related offences (*The Guardian*, 27 September 1999). As the semi-official Vatican newspaper *Osservatore Romano* put it: 'In a few seconds seven years of inquiry and the declarations of a dozen *pentiti* have collapsed. The 'supergrassocracy' has been swept away'(*The Guardian*, 27 September 1999). The new millennium has, therefore, dawned in Italy, with the mafia weakened, but not defeated, and with the credibility of the *pentiti* as a legitimate and viable method of dealing with it in serious doubt.

## Political violence

### The supergrass process in Northern Ireland

The supergrass process emerged in Northern Ireland in the early 1980s as part of a series of law enforcement initiatives introduced from the late 1960s to address the problem of political violence (Greer, 1995). Its appearance stemmed from three principal factors: the maturing and refinement of the counter-terrorist intelligence-gathering system throughout the previous decade, the difficulties the police faced in obtaining confessions from key suspects following restrictions on anti-terrorist interrogation methods in 1979, and a crisis of allegiance amongst certain paramilitary activists, especially those who, by the early 1980s, had already served one period of imprisonment and, having been arrested again, could not face another. The suspension of the regional administration at Stormont, in March 1972, enabled the UK government to implement reforms, not the least of which was the Northern Ireland (Emergency Provisions) Act 1973. Designed to modify the criminal justice process to enable internment without trial to be discontinued, the Act instituted a confession-based prosecution process centred around non-jury single-judge courts, serviced by extensive police and army powers to stop and question, search and seize and arrest and detain, which remains substantially unaltered to this day (Boyle, *et al*; 1980; Walsh, 1983).

When internment was finally phased out in 1975 the 'Diplock process'[4] became the principal vehicle for countering terrorism through prosecution and conviction on the basis of confessions obtained in special anti-terrorist police interrogation centres. In the late 1970s there was a flood of complaints about the physical abuse of police detainees (*Bennett Report*, 1979: app.2). But these dropped dramatically in 1979 following publication of the report by the Bennett Inquiry which made a series of recommendations to limit the scope for maltreatment, such as regular breaks in questioning, medical checks, improved rights of access to legal advice, and the monitoring of interviews by other police officers on CCTV (*Bennett Report*; Boyle *et al*, 1980: 40).

The Bennett reforms appear to have made the extraction of confessions more difficult especially in the case of committed members of paramilitary organisations resilient enough to withstand the psychological pressure which the police can legally apply. Coinciding with these developments, a series of security disasters in 1979 prompted the first serious attempt by the government to rationalise intelligence-gathering which, in spite of its considerable sophistication, had been plagued throughout the decade by duplication of effort and by rivalry and mistrust between the various agencies involved. The decision to 'turn' key paramilitary activists to work for the authorities, and to persuade them to turn Queen's evidence, was one of the consequences of this reorganisation (Urban, 1992: 133). Although a supergrass process of the kind which emerged could not have been actively planned at this stage – particularly since the supply of supergrasses was highly unpredictable – it was a short step from recruiting highly placed informers to developing a system for their appearance as witnesses in court.

The supergrass process began hesitantly with two comparatively modest trials in 1981 and experienced a brief ascendancy in 1983 when most of the accused were convicted, largely without corroboration, in three important cases featuring loyalist renegade Joseph Bennett, and IRA turncoats Christopher Black and Kevin McGrady. At its height some 25 supergrasses were responsible for the arrest of nearly 600 suspects. As in England, immunity from prosecution was offered as a reward in the early stages, but, in response to public criticism, was replaced by reduced sentences and the promise of new identities after these had been served. Over half the supergrasses retracted their evidence, leaving ten principal trials involving over 200 defendants.

The process was highly controversial and, unusually for Northern Ireland, the debate transcended the traditional sectarian divide. Of particular concern, especially to independent observers, was the fact that Diplock trials undermined the traditional common law rule requiring trial judges to warn juries about the dangers of convicting on accomplice evidence without corroboration. A judicial U-turn occurred after the discrediting of Jackie Grimley in the fourth supergrass trial in 1983.

Convictions were secured purely on the supergrasses' testimony in only two of the remaining seven trials at first instance. In the others the defendants were either acquitted, or convicted on confessions and supergrass evidence combined, although the confessions alone would legally have sufficed. The process was over by 1986.[5] Following the five appeal hearings, the only convictions to remain extant were those based on confessions or an alleged admission, an overall conviction rate of only 24 per cent. While it initially appeared to constitute a radical departure from the original basis of the Diplock system, the supergrass process in Northern Ireland turned out to be merely a fresh means for identifying defendants, obtaining confessions and ensuring that certain key suspects were remanded in custody, which, in a handful of cases, lasted for up to four years as those concerned were shunted from one supergrass to another before eventually being acquitted or having their convictions quashed.

The impact of the supergrass process on the level of political violence in Northern Ireland in the mid-1980s was, at best, marginal and short-lived. The terrorist murder rate, to take just one indicator, shows two high peaks in 1972 (467) and 1976 (297), followed immediately by steep declines, with much smaller rises in 1979 (113) and 1981 (101), followed by a drop from 97 in 1982 to 54 in 1985 and then a rise from 61 in 1986 to 93 in both 1987 and 1988. The trough, therefore, roughly coincides with the supergrass years and may be at least partly attributable to the arrest of large numbers of active members of paramilitary organisations on supergrass evidence. But it may also have been influenced by other developments, such as the more careful targeting of victims and the political rise of Sinn Fein in the aftermath of the prison protests in the late 70s and early 80s.

While the Diplock courts continued routinely to convict on confession evidence, the demise of the supergrass process in 1986 left a hiatus in anti-terrorist law enforcement in Northern Ireland. A familiar complaint was suddenly revived as a justification for further legislative change; guilty terrorists were using the right to remain silent in police interrogation to evade lawful conviction. In spite of the fact that this argument had been rejected twice by government following two official inquiries in England in the early 1970s and early 80s, without further discussion or deliberation the Criminal Evidence (Northern Ireland) Order 1988 was passed by parliament (Greer, 1990; Jackson, 1989).

This legislation permits courts in Northern Ireland to draw inferences from the silence of defendants where: (a) in the course of police questioning before being charged, they refrained from offering an explanation which subsequently formed part of their defence at trial, or, upon being charged, they declined to mention any fact they could 'reasonably have been expected to mention' to the police; (b) upon being called by the court to give evidence they either refused to be sworn, or having been sworn, declined 'without good cause' to answer any question; (c) while under arrest they failed or refused to account for an 'object, substance or mark' reasonably believed by the police to be connected with the offence; and (d) while under arrest they failed to account for their presence at the place where, and around the time at which, the offence was alleged to have been committed, and the police reasonably believe they were there in connection with it. The Order also expressly allows such silences to be treated as corroboration of other evidence (Articles 3(2)(c)(ii), 4(4)(b), 5(2)(ii), 6(2)(ii)).

In 1984 the Northern Ireland Court of Appeal had criticised the trial judge in the Bennett case for concluding that the credibility of the supergrass evidence was strengthened by the failure of the defendants to testify in their own defence. The Lord Chief Justice held that, in such circumstances, it was difficult to accept that the evidence of a 'suspect witness' could ever be so compelling that the accused would be required to testify under pain of certain prejudice (*R v Graham* (1984) 18 *NIJB*: 19–22). The 1988 Order appeared to presage a revived supergrass process in which informer evidence would be corroborated by the silence of defendants in any of the four circumstances provided. But this did not happen, apparently because of serious doubts about whether the courts, having repudiated convictions on uncorroborated supergrass evidence, would regard silence in police interrogation as sufficiently corroborative. Although the Northern Ireland Court of Appeal had been careful not to exclude entirely the possibility of conviction on uncorroborated supergrass evidence, it had affirmed not only the importance of corroboration, but also that it should generally be of a particularly compelling kind in such cases (Greer, 1995: 253–6).

## The Italian anti-terrorist *pentiti* process

The construction of a *pentiti* process against the armed left in Italy began with the reorganisation of the intelligence-gathering system in the mid-1970s, followed by the enactment of a series of temporary laws designed to encourage terrorists to collaborate with the authorities (Greer, 1995: 234–9). The first of these was passed in March 1978 just a week after former Prime Minister Aldo Moro, Italy's elder statesman, was kidnapped by the Red Brigades. In addition to the creation of several new offences, including the crime of 'terrorism or subversion of the democratic order' (Law N. 191, 21 March 1978), it also contained new intelligence-gathering provisions (for the tapping of telephones, for example), and extra police powers to detain for identity checks and to conduct interrogations without a lawyer present. Radically reduced sentences of 2–4 years were offered to terrorist kidnappers who dissociated themselves from their organisation and helped locate and free hostages. In 1979 the so-called '7 April trial' began with some 200 defendants charged with subversion and membership of armed bands, and by 1984 4,000 suspects were being held on remand in connection with these proceedings (*The Guardian*, 9 August 1984; Amnesty International, 1986). However, one of the key witnesses, *pentito* Carlo Fioroni, eventually absconded without testifying in the main trial.

The role of *pentiti* was augmented by further legislation when the Cossiga Act (Law N.15 of 15 February 1980) was passed in February 1980 making it an offence, punishable with prison sentences of up to 15 years, to join, promote, constitute, organise, or direct an association which sought to subvert the democratic order by violent means. Article 4 provided for the reduction of prison sentences in respect of defendants who, having been found guilty of terrorist acts, dissociated themselves from their comrades and did all they could to prevent the continuation of criminal activity 'by giving concrete help to the police and magistrates in establishing decisive proof leading to the identification and arrest of conspirators'. Article 5 stipulated that immunity from punishment could be obtained by those who not only collaborated with the authorities in order to prevent crimes against the democratic state, but also provided substantial evidence regarding conspiracies, including details of how exactly the crime was organised, and the identification of other conspirators. Radically reduced prison terms were also offered to those found guilty of belonging to terrorist organisations, provided they were willing to dissociate, renounce their terrorist activities, and help the authorities.

By the early 1980s the *pentiti* process had decimated right-wing terrorism, hundreds of left wing suspects had been arrested, and entire leftist organisations had been dismantled. While the frequency of terrorist incidents declined, police officers, *pentiti*, and their families increasingly became targets. In an attempt to regain the initiative the Red Brigades kidnapped American General and NATO officer James Dozier from his home in Verona on 18 December 1982. But in January 1983, acting upon information obtained from informers, the police stormed the hideout and secured the General's release. Further arrests followed when the leader of the Dozier kidnap, Antonio Savasta, himself 'repented' and when many of those he implicated also turned states evidence.

The success of the Cossiga Act prompted the Italian legislature to pass a further temporary *pentiti* statute (Law N. 304 of 29 May 1982), lasting until February 1983. Immunity from prosecution was offered to those who had committed, or attempted to commit, minor crimes. Reduced penalties were made available to those guilty of more serious offences provided they dissociated themselves from their former activities, made full confession and helped to reduce the impact of their wrong-doing. Penalties attaching to more serious offences were further reduced for those who confessed and took part in a reconstruction of the crime, or helped the police and judicial authorities to obtain crucial evidence leading to the capture of other offenders. Reduced sentences for terrorists who had 'collaborated in a very decisive way' were also made available, and the legislation also provided for a possible review of a court decision to reduce a penalty when the statement upon which it had been based turned out to be false. Another Act was passed in February 1987 which required dissociation, confession, repudiation and reformation as the conditions for the reduction of penalties but which made no mention of active collaboration in the judicial process (Law N. 34 of 18 February 1987). However, no attempt was made in the 1980s to protect the political *pentiti* in the manner of the Witness Protection Program of the United States, or even the less formal arrangements found in the supergrass system in Northern Ireland (*Sunday Times* colour supplement, 4 September 1984).

By 29 January 1983, 389 terrorists had taken advantage of the *pentiti* laws and repented. Although Red Brigades trials continued into the 1990s (*The Guardian*, 21 April 1990) the evidence supplied by *pentiti*, 'along with the anti-terrorist apparatus put in place after the Moro assassination, brought an end to Italy's second episode of terrorist violence' (Weinberg and Eubank, 1987: 130). The success of the Italian *'pentiti* strategy' against terrorist organisations stemmed from a conjunction of 'supply' and 'demand' factors similar to those found in the supergrass system in Northern Ireland. On the demand side were arrangements for effective intelligence-gathering, severe sentences for those who refused to cooperate, and the prospect of clemency for those who did. A crisis of allegiance within the insurrectionary movement itself provided an abundant supply of willing collaborators (Guerri, 1983). The fact that Italian terrorism had a much narrower social base than its Irish equivalent was also an important factor.

## German *staatszeugen*

Informer evidence was also used, to a modest extent, in Germany in the 1980s and 90s, in trials of those accused of right-and left-wing terrorism (Greer, 1995: 242–5). Although, in May 1975, the prosecution case against the four founding members of the Red Army Faction (or Baader-Meinhof gang)[6] hinged upon the testimony of their one-time associate, Gerhard Müller who turned states evidence, it was not until the mid-1980s that a number of trials of leading neo-Nazi activists occurred in which accomplice evidence was of systematic importance. Writing in the late 1980s Kolinsky concluded that 'a mixture of trying to save one's bacon and getting into the limelight and the media may explain why, in contrast to their colleagues on the left, right-wing terrorists have tended to name their accomplices, and divulge information about their organisations and activities during police interrogations' (Kolinsky, 1988; Hasselbach, 1996).

With the demolition of the Berlin wall and the re-unification of Germany in 1989, a number of Red Army Faction suspects who had enjoyed the protection of the East German secret police (the Stasi) were arrested in the newly unified state. In June 1989 the West German legislature introduced a new temporary scheme, lapsing in 1992, which enabled several to be recruited as *staatszeugen* (state witnesses) in return for greatly reduced prison sentences (Nr. 26 Tag der Ausgabe: Bonn, 15 Juni 1989). The Federal Prosecutor-General was authorised, with the approval of a criminal panel of the Federal Court of Justice, to refrain from prosecution if a party guilty of a terrorist offence revealed facts to the prosecuting authorities which were likely to prevent such an offence being committed, help solve it, or lead to the arrest of the offenders (s.1). Where prosecution had been initiated, the court was empowered to refrain from sentencing altogether, or to mitigate punishment, at its discretion (s.2). *Staatszeugen* charged with murder or manslaughter were entitled to be considered for a reduced sentence, but not immunity from prosecution, while those charged with genocide were excluded from the scheme altogether (s.3). The prosecuting authorities were permitted to stay proceedings, and the courts to refrain from sentencing or to impose lighter sentences, in respect of state witnesses who provided significant evidence likely to be of assistance in the prevention of offences more serious than those in which they themselves had been involved, and which also implicated those more culpable.

The *staatszeugen* process was criticised at the time on familiar grounds; that the evidence lacked credibility, there was no corroboration requirement, the legitimacy of the criminal justice system could be damaged by the appearance of a deal being struck with criminals, and it was of doubtful efficacy (Vercher, 1992: 284). However, unlike the high profile informer-evidence processes considered elsewhere in this study, the German variant was small in scale and directed at a virtually moribund organisation representing little threat. Indeed, in April 1992, the Red Army Faction announced an end to its twenty-year struggle, admitted its own 'mistakes' and stated that it recognised the 'fundamental changes' which had occurred 'in global politics over the past few years' (*The Guardian*, 21 April 1992).

## Spanish *arepentidos* and French *repentis*

Finally it is worth noting that, although legislation was enacted in Spain and France in the mid-1980s to encourage 'repentant' members of terrorist organisations to collaborate with the authorities, this did not result in the development of a trial process on the evidence of Spanish *arepentidos* or French *repentis* (Vercher, 1992: ch.9). In Spain a more attractive, and highly successful, alternative was also available: the re-integration, by exercise of the executive pardon, of members of terrorist organisations not involved in serious crimes of violence who formally promised not to re-offend (Vercher, 1992: 268–9, 271–2, 275). Although no formal legal arrangements were made for the protection of informers, French police funds for their remuneration were increased, and the Ministries of the Interior and of Justice provided the same kind of informal protection as that offered to supergrasses and their families in Northern Ireland, such as changes of identity, occupation and residence (Cacciani and Bonetti, 1987: 79, 95). Together with other measures, these arrangements seem to have been sufficient to deal with French terrorism (except in Corsica) without a supergrass process.

## Conclusion

Three factors were particularly influential in the emergence of the processes considered in this study at the times and places concerned:

- the maturing of intelligence and informer systems to the point where sufficient information became available to identify potential supergrasses and defendants;

- the actual or perceived failure of other methods employed to tackle organised political or non-political crime;

- the desire to capitalise one last time on the services of an informer whose cover had been blown, or to exploit crises of allegiance on the part of members of target organisations under arrest who had not hitherto been used as informers.

Several other distinctions, in addition to that between political and non-political crime, can be made. An obvious contrast is between those processes which made an effective contribution to crime control (the US Witness Protection Program and the anti-terrorist processes in Italy and Germany) and those which did not (the Northern Irish anti-terrorist and the Italian anti-mafia experiments). While supergrasses may have been used in England with some success against bank robbery and related offences in the early 1970s, their limitations soon became apparent when their inherent unreliability was exposed, and when the activities of criminal organisations shifted to activities which limited their role.

A second distinction can be found between those processes rooted in legislation (the US Witness Protection Program, and the Italian and German anti-terrorist processes), and the remainder which were grafted on to existing legal arrangements. Legislation tends to confer a higher level of democratic legitimacy, provides more carefully constructed checks and balances, and offers better prospects of enduring success. A third distinction can be drawn between the English process, which, in spite of a controversial infancy, was accommodated within the regular criminal justice system for several years before its decline, and the Italian anti-mafia and Northern Irish anti-terrorist variants which were never successfully institutionalised because of irresolvable doubts about their compatibility with due process standards. In Northern Ireland these concerns inspired a well-orchestrated campaign against conviction by single judge courts on uncorroborated supergrass evidence which precipitated the demise of the supergrass process within a few years of its inception. As for the Italian anti-mafia process, the controversy has spanned a decade and a half and has, as yet, not been definitatively resolved.

Effective inter-agency coordination is vital for the success of supergrass processes and this is also best achieved by legislation. The key institutions are the police and the courts. The courts must be prepared to convict on supergrass evidence, even if they also require corroboration, and to trust the police assessment of the utility of the service the supergrass has provided. Legislation can generally provide clearer, and more democratically legitimate, guidelines than the courts can produce themselves. Supergrass processes are based upon proactive intelligence-led policing and the police bear the responsibility of making the preliminary decision about who to recruit and who to prosecute. It is also clear that, a few genuine conversions aside, what motivates supergrasses most is self-interest, particularly the prospect of leniency in, or the avoidance of, punishment. The rewards available to those from both terrorist and organised crime backgrounds are characteristically, the most generous any criminal justice system is prepared to offer informants. This can include immunity from prosecution; an extremely lenient prison sentence and comparative luxury while serving it; money; and new lives with fresh identities (apparently in modest circumstances) away from the original sphere of operations. Employing the services of supergrasses is a high-risk strategy since, if it succeeds, the punishment of dozens, if not hundreds, of suspects is assured. But if it fails, a valuable source of intelligence plus considerable resources will have been squandered, exposing the police and criminal justice system to criticism for having preferred crime control short-cuts over the more long-term gains which may be obtained by observance of due process values.

The author would like to thank Paul Fitzsimmons and Fabio Biffi for providing some useful background information relating to the US and Italy respectively.

# Notes

1 It is said that the nickname 'grass' stems from 'grasshopper' for 'copper' (policeman) but it may also owe something to the popular song *Whispering Grass* and to the phrase 'snake in the grass'.

2 Between 1 January 1979 and June 1982 there were 18 supergrasses ('resident informers') in the Metropolitan Police district (Letter of 21 June 1982 to Christopher Price MP from the Home Secretary, cited in Seymour, 1982).

3 Corrupt police officers were used as supergrasses in an anti-corruption drive by the Metropolitan police in the late 1990s, but one was dropped in March 2000 due to doubts about the reliability of his evidence (*The Guardian*, 20 March 2000 and 6 April 2000). 'Witness protection is, however, a growth industry. In recent years four police forces – Scotland Yard, Manchester, Merseyside, and Northumbria – have set up units with a formalised procedure to help vulnerable witnesses, possibly moving them and giving them new identities.' (Bellos, 1996).

4 Named after Lord Diplock who chaired the commission of inquiry whose recommendations were largely enacted in the Northern Ireland (Emergency Provisions) Act 1973.

5 However, the story was revisited in the late 1990s when two former supergrasses published their memoirs (Collins with McGovern, 1997 and Gilmour, 1998). Collins, who lived openly in Newry in Northern Ireland, died in suspicious circumstances on 27 January 1999. Gilmour is a permanent fugitive whose whereabouts are unknown. Two other IRA informers have also published their memoirs (McGartland, 1997 and O'Callaghan, 1998). McGarland, who had gone into hiding, was shot and seriously wounded outside his Tyneside home on 17 June 1999.

6 Andreas Baader, Ulrike Meinhof, Jan Karl Raspe and Gudrun Ensslin.

# References

Alexander, S. (1989) *The Pizza Connection – Lawyers, drugs and the mafia*, London: W.H. Allen.

'The Bennett Report' (1979), *Report of the Committee of Inquiry into Police Interrogation Procedures in Northern Ireland*, Cmnd. 7497, London: HMSO.

Bellos A. (1996) 'Nowhere Men', *The Guardian/The Guide*, 17-23 August.

Blumenthal R. (1989) *Last Days of the Sicilians: At War with the Mafia – The FBI Assault on the Pizza Connection*, London: Bloomsbury.

Boyle K. Hadden T. and Hillyard P. (1980) *Ten Years on in Northern Ireland: The Legal Control of Political Violence*, London: The Cobden Trust.

Cacciani M. and Bonetti M. (1987) *'Normativa antiterrorismo e nuovi modelli di organizzazione precessuale nell'esperienza francese' in* Milan: Centro Nazionale di Prevenzione e Difesa Sociale.

Campbell D. (1991) 'Whisper Who Dares', *Police Review*: 532.

Campbell D. (1994) 'The Underworld', London: BBC Books.

Centro Nazionale di Prevenzione e Difensa Sociale (1987) *Convenzione per una recerca su 'Normative ed esperienze di maxiprocessi e sulla utilizzabilita e gestibilita probatoria dei c. d. testimoni della corona e della relative tutela. Confronto con l'esperienza itiliana.' Rapporto finale I & II*, Milan: Centro Nazionale di Prevenzione e Difesa Sociale.

Collins E. with McGovern M. (1997) *Killing Rage*, London: Granta Books.

Criminal Law Revision Committee (1972), *Eleventh Report, Evidence General*, Cmnd. 4991, London: HMSO.

Falcone G. and Padovani M. (1992) *Men of Honour: The Truth About the Mafia*, London: Warner Books.

Gilmour R. (1998) *Dead Ground: Infiltrating the IRA*, London: Little Brown.

Greer S. (1990) 'The Right to Silence: A Review of the Current Debate', *53 Modern Law Review, 709.*

Greer S. (1995) Supergrasses: *A Study in anti-terrorist law enforcement in Northern Ireland*, Oxford: Clarendon Press.

Guerri G.B. (1983) *'P.Peci, io, l'infamy'*, Milan: Mondotori.

Hasselbach, I. with Reiss, T. (1996) *Führer – Ex: Memoirs of a Former Neo-nazi*, London: Chatto & Windus.

Jackson, J. (1989) 'Recent Developments in Criminal Evidence', *40 Northern Ireland Legal Quarterly:* 105.

Kolinsky, E. (1988) 'Terrorism in West Germany', *in* J. Lodge (ed). *The Threat of Terrorism*, Brighton: Wheatsheaf.

Lawson, R.J. (1992) 'Lying, cheating and stealing at government expense: striking a balance between the public interest and the interests of the public in the Witness Protection Program', *24 Arizona State Law Journal*: 1429.

Levin, J.M. (1985) 'Organised Crime and Insulated Violence: Federal liability for Illegal Conduct in the Witness Protection Program', 76 *Journal of Criminal Law and Criminology*: 208.

Maas, P. (1987) *Underboss: Sammy the Bull Gravano's Story of Life in the Mafia*, London: Harper Collins.

Mark R. (1972) 'The Disease of Crime: punishment or treatment'? (Lecture to Royal Society of Medicine, London: 6,13).

McGartland, M. (1997) *Fifty Dead Men Walking*, London: Blake Publishing.

Morton, J. (1995) *Supergrasses and Informers: an informal history of undercover police work*, London: Warner Books.

O'Callaghan, S. (1998) *The Informer*, London: Bantham Press.

O'Mahoney, M. with Woodind, D. (1978) *King Squealer: The True Story of Maurice O'Mahoney*, London: Sphere Books.

Radzinowicz, L. (1956) *A History of English Criminal Law and its Administration from 1750*, Vol. II, London: Steven.

Seymour, D. (1982) 'What good have supergrasses done for anyone but themselves?', *Legal Action Group Bulletin*, December: 9.

Shawcross, T. and Young, M. (1988) *Mafia Wars – the Confessions of Tommaso Buscetta*, London: Fontana.

Stille, A. (1995) *Excellent Cadavers: the Mafia and the death of the first Italian republic*, London: Jonathan Cape.

Urban, M. (1992) *Big Boys' Rules: the SAS and the secret struggle against the IRA*, London: Faber & Faber.

Vercher, A. (1992) *Terrorism in Europe: an international comparative legal analysis*, Oxford: Clarendon Press.

Walsh, D. P. J. (1983) *The Use and Abuse of Emergency Legislation in Northern Ireland*, London: The Cobden Trust.

Weinberg, L. and Eubank, W.L. (1987) *The Rise and Fall of Italian Terrorism*, Boulder, Colorado: Westview Press.

## Cases cited

*R. v Davies and Gorman* (1978) 68 Cr.App.R. 319.

*R. v Graham* (1984) 18 Northern Ireland Judgment Bulletin.

*R. v King* (1985) Crim. L.R. 748.

*R. v Lowe* (1978) 66 Cr. App. R. 122.

*R. v Preston* (1987) 9 Cr.App. R. (S.) 155.

*R. v Rose & Sapiano* (1980) 2 Cr.App.R. (S.) 239.

*R. v Sinfield* (1981) 3 Cr. App R. (S.) 258.

*R. v Thorne* (1978) 66 Cr. App R.6.

*R. v Tremarco* (1978) 1 Cr.App.R. (S.) 286.

*R. v Turner* (1975) Cr. App.R.67.

# 9 Managing anonymous informants through Crimestoppers

## Bill Griffiths and Alan Murphy

> 'ANONYMOUS INFORMATION ABOUT CRIME
> COULD EARN A CASH REWARD
> PHONE FREE ON 0800 555 111'

The advertising industry would call this the 'drinking chocolate message' – it tells you what Crimestoppers is or does. Indeed, if you

*have* information about crime

*and* you wish to remain anonymous to the criminal justice system

*and* wish to provide that information to the police for action,

this simple message tells you all you need to know to make that happen. The same message is written on the ceiling of every police cell in London.

The purpose of this chapter is to set out the relevance and importance of Crimestoppers to the informer system, including the operating context, the history of its development, and the challenges it poses to management.

## Crimestoppers in context

> Crime undermines basic freedoms, particularly the freedom to live one's life free from fear and intimidation. As a society, we cannot stand back from this. But Government action alone cannot solve the problem. Government needs to create the conditions in which individuals and communities themselves take the initiative, to take control of their neighbourhoods for the benefit of all. If we can cut crime, reduce the fear of crime, we can add value to every aspect of life. Reducing crime and the fear of crime enhances liberty and revitalises communities.
>
> (Home Office, 1999)

Crimestoppers addresses the heart of this aspiration by offering, as it does, freedom from fear of retribution because the anonymity guarantee reassures the caller that 'no one will ever know you phoned'. The essential message from Crimestoppers to the community is that they *can* seize the initiative and take control of their neighbourhoods by the simple act of picking up the telephone and dialling the freephone number.

> We can and must make an impact on crime. Intelligence-led policing and partnership initiatives are the way forward.
>
> ('The London Beat', 1998: 11)

Crimestoppers is a prime source of intelligence in that it captures information that would not otherwise be available from the people that hold the information the police need in order to be effective. Moreover, the use of detectives to receive the calls has proved to be the best way of ensuring that corroboration and opportunities are identified so that action upon anonymous information is both feasible and legal. The philosophy is that intelligence translated into action leads to detections, so the detection of crime and prosecution of offenders will contribute to crime reduction. In 'Best Value' terms, the cost of Crimestoppers is more than justified by the results achieved.

Crimestoppers is a classic partnership that depends on three elements for sustenance and growth. Firstly, Crimestoppers is supported by a registered charity, the Crimestoppers Trust, the only charity that actually leads to the charging of offenders. Money is raised locally and nationally from business and other communities to promote the scheme, to pay for development managers and for the rewards to be paid to informants that claim them. Uniquely, these rewards are managed by non-police volunteers. The introduction of the Crime and Disorder Act 1998 has provided an ideal vehicle for Crimestoppers to be incorporated with local partnerships based on local authority areas, particularly as a means of mobilising communities in high crime neighbourhoods.

Secondly, Crimestoppers' success depends entirely on communication and an understanding of the key message. Without the support of the media, communication would be prohibitively costly and understanding dangerously limited. The response to appeals, both specific and general, has proved to be highly effective when targeted at the audience most likely to be in a position to respond – the people who hold the information the police desire.

Thirdly, in order to deliver the results that informants are entitled to expect, it is essential that the police service provide adequate, appropriately skilled resources to receive and screen the anonymous calls. The anonymous information must then be developed into actionable intelligence in order to achieve arrests that lead to the charging of offender(s) with criminal offences.

Loss or degradation of any of these elements would seriously undermine the Crimestoppers contribution to the crime strategy.

# Why is Crimestoppers necessary?

People have a variety of reasons for demanding their identity be protected, and the principle of protecting the identity of informants for the greater good of society has long been a tenet of English law. Moreover, there are now witness protection schemes to promote confidence that citizens who come forward in the face of risk can be afforded protection by the criminal justice system (see chapter 10 on Witness Protection). But for some these safeguards are insufficient or are not trusted; the risks in coming forward may be too high. Broadly, there are three groups of informers who are attracted by the Crimestoppers offer of anonymity. They are as follows:

- criminals who have information on the activities of other criminals but do not wish to be identified as an informer;

- family members of criminals, wives, girlfriends and other close associates of the criminal who have information but do not wish to compromise the relationship or harbour fear of reprisal;

- and members of the general public who are not themselves criminals or associated with crime, yet have information on criminal activity and do not want to get involved by being seen contacting or talking to police.

Typically, the latter group live in close proximity to the criminal or their activities and fear retribution on themselves or their families if their name is revealed.

Without the facility of Crimestoppers these groups have little prospect of being heard. An anonymous call can be made direct to the police but the response to unevaluated information is likely to have low priority and poor support. There is also the risk to the caller that they will be recorded and thus disclosed if action leads to the charge of an offender.

If Crimestoppers had not been valued by such groups the scheme could not have flourished. It began with a London launch in 1988 and by 1998 it covered the whole of the British Isles. Our evidence suggests many Crimestoppers informers have progressed into the conventional informant management system. They develop trust in the trained officers who receive the initial call and thereafter grow more confident in the protection afforded by mainstream informer control. These 'managed' informants may never have been introduced without the Crimestoppers route being available.

## The development of Crimestoppers

Crimestoppers was conceived by Greg MacAleese, a detective in Albuquerque, New Mexico, USA in 1976. In July that year a university student was working a late shift at a small petrol station in the town. It was two weeks before his wedding. That night two men robbed the station and senselessly shot and killed him. This robbery was the culmination of a series of armed robberies against petrol stations, which MacAleese thought had been committed by local people, and he believed that someone within the local community knew who was responsible. However, nobody was willing to talk to the police and after six weeks he still had no leads.

He then devised the notion of a telephone 'hotline' which anyone could ring and pass on information anonymously. He persuaded local businessmen to fund a reward, and the local media to broadcast the appeal and publicise details of the telephone line, guaranteeing that the caller would remain anonymous. Anonymity was entirely new. Within 72 hours an informer had phoned with specific information which led directly to the arrest and conviction of the two offenders for murder. In addition, Detective MacAleese received information about a number of other unsolved crimes along with information on criminal activity within the community of which the police were completely unaware.

This new concept quickly spread in schemes across the USA and into Canada as well as Australia to the point where international conferences were held and UK interest attracted. Crimestoppers is fully endorsed by the US Department of Justice and the Federal Bureau of Investigation.

Crimestoppers was introduced into the UK as a proposal for development during the mid-1980s, the first local scheme being founded in Kings Lynn with support from the local newspaper. The Metropolitan Police Service subsequently launched the first dedicated Crimestoppers scheme in January 1988. They were also responsible for organising the charity which funds the umbrella partnership, the Community Action Trust now the Crimestoppers Trust, with substantial help in funding from a group of businessmen.

The Crimestoppers Unit, staffed by detectives at New Scotland Yard, was originally set up to encourage anonymous information with respect to serious violent crime. The original media partnership was with Thames Television so, although based in London, the Scotland Yard unit received telephone calls on the 0800 555 111 freephone number for the whole south-east of England.

Within ten years, twenty-nine Crimestoppers partnerships had been formed, ranging from large conurbations like London and Manchester to county schemes in Staffordshire and Wiltshire, to a countrywide scheme in Scotland. They are all supported by the Trust which is responsible for overall development and national promotions such as the SNAP ('Say No to Drugs and Phone') campaign.

The trustees have set up an advisory group to advance a business plan to secure the future of the scheme nationally. They run an annual conference that embraces all elements of the partnership. There are regular professional meetings for police co-ordinators and a working group of senior police representatives reports to the ACPO (Association of Chief Police Officers) Intelligence Committee.

## The significance of anonymity

Crimestoppers is unique because of its offer and guarantee of anonymity. The preservation of this guarantee is therefore vital to future success. The Criminal Procedure and Investigations Act 1996 introduced a statutory framework for the disclosure of unused material. Crimestoppers intelligence reports are unused sensitive material as defined by the Act. Although Crimestoppers does not ask the informer any identifying details, the nature of the information provided can often be enough to identify the source. The existence of Crimestoppers intelligence reports are not be made known to the offender under any circumstances. The officer in charge of the investigation and/or disclosure officer has a responsibility to ensure that all material, including Crimestoppers intelligence reports, obtained in the course of a criminal investigation and which may be relevant to the investigation is retained.

Should the disclosure officer consider that the Crimestoppers material falls within either test for disclosure, the material will be supplied to the Crown Prosecution Service. A statement will be prepared by the police in support of either disclosure of unused material, or an application for public interest immunity will be made. The key ingredient of the Crimestoppers scheme is its promise of anonymity. Therefore, any actions to trace the identity of the informant must be resisted at all times. The integrity of the promise of anonymity must be paramount in order to ensure that nothing should undermine the effectiveness of the scheme. So much so, that the Crown Prosecution Service are prepared to argue that the public interest in protecting the scheme means that any suggestion of tracing the informer would not be a reasonable line of enquiry. It follows that voice recordings should be avoided. In addition, the facility to trace telephone calls back to point of origin should be inhibited on the telephone system for the Crimestoppers unit.

## Rewards

Cash rewards are available through the Crimestoppers scheme. A Crimestoppers reward can be paid to anyone who gives information on the Crimestoppers freephone telephone number which leads to the arrest and charge of a suspect for a crime. Unlike most conventional reward payments, the trial or conviction of a suspect is not a prerequisite for payment. In this context, 'charge' means an offence cleared up on current Home Office guidelines, including the issue of a formal caution. When a suspect is released on police bail pending a decision by the Crown Prosecution Service whether or not to bring charges, then for the purposes of a Crimestoppers reward this may be considered a charge made, and is a matter for the local Board to consider.

The maximum reward available is up to £500 for each separate incident, regardless of the number of arrests or charges. This relatively modest reward is designed to be less attractive to the professional informer, but it must also be remembered that the money comes from charitable subscriptions, not public funding. However, the Crimestoppers Trust also offer specified rewards (usually up to £5,000) from centrally managed funds in specific cases which can be of particular help to the senior investigating officer in a protracted murder investigation.

Reward payments are carried out without prejudice to the caller's anonymity by means of a unique reference number (URN) issued to the caller by the Crimestoppers office. When an arrest and charge is made, and it is known that the caller seeks a reward, the local Crimestoppers Board will facilitate payment through a bank using the URN.

In contrast to the position in the USA, it is interesting to note that the experience of Crimestoppers in the UK to date is that few informers actually want to claim a reward. This may be because the Crimestoppers informer, although accepting that his or her anonymity is guaranteed while on the telephone, may not believe that they can actually collect a reward payment and remain anonymous at the same time. On the other hand, it may be that informers' main motivation is simply to see that offenders are brought to justice.

In any event, as seen in Table 9.1 below, statistics collated nationally show that proportionately fewer rewards are being paid out through Crimestoppers each year.

## The contribution of Crimestoppers to the informant system

Although every effort is made to preserve anonymity, officers receiving calls are also trained to encourage the informer if the dialogue suggests this may be possible or, as is frequently the case, trust is built up over time. Clearly, the handling of informers calls for the judgement and training of an experienced officer. Objectivity in evaluating both the informer and the information is essential, notwithstanding the strong personal relationship that may develop between the informer and handler. These attributes are essential in a Crimestoppers officer.

**Table 9.1**  *Crimestoppers: arrests and rewards 1996–1998*

|  | 1996 | 1997 | 1998 |
|---|---|---|---|
| Arrests | 4347 | 4726 | 5169 |
| Positive calls | 44,424 | 48,385 | 54,451 |
| Rewards paid | 631 | 420 | 309 |
| Amount paid in reward (not enhanced rewards) | £75,089 | £44,195 | £40,785 |
| Calls per arrest | 10.2 | 10.2 | 10.5 |
| Arrests per reward | 6.89 | 11.3 | 16.7 |
| Calls per reward | 70.4 | 115.2 | 176.2 |
| Average reward | £119 | £105 | £132 |
| % claiming rewards | 15% | 9% | 6% |

*Source*: Crimestoppers Trust, unpublished report.

An introduction to the conventional management of an informer consistent with the ACPO National Guidelines on the Use and Management of informants can be achieved without compromise to the anonymity offered by Crimestoppers. A Crimestoppers URN would be issued to the informant in the normal manner and then the informant is introduced by an agreed method to a named operational handler outside the Crimestoppers unit. The informer will then become known to the handler and not to the Crimestoppers officer and may be managed thereafter without compromise in either direction.

The circumstances which could lead to such an introduction include the following:

- a Crimestoppers informer seeking more substantial payment than paid by the Crimestoppers Board;

- an informer close to the offender could be detained at the same time as a result of the informer's own information;

- an informer who could be considered to be bordering on participation in crime and would benefit from management within the guidelines in order to proceed;

- it is apparent that the safety and welfare of the informer is being placed at exceptional risk and the informant would therefore require extra levels of protection;

- it is apparent that the informer has regular and close access to information on criminal activity and it would be in the interests of crime detection and prevention to task the informant accordingly within the guidelines;

- where the information is of a complex and sensitive nature and an introduction could significantly facilitate the investigation if the informer were to deal direct with an investigating officer;

- the informer has access to, and is in a position to produce and iden- tify documentary and/or physical evidence, the evidential integrity of which would be lost or undermined if submitted anonymously.

These examples are not exhaustive but experience has shown them to be the main reasons for seeking the introduction of a Crimestoppers informer into the mainstream managed system. Although doing this is at the discretion and judgement of the Crimestoppers officer, the Crimestoppers informer is always in a position to choose to remain anonymous.

Table 9.2 below provides evidence of Crimestoppers 'added value' to the Metropolitan Police Service informer system by the introduction of initially anonymous individuals.

**Table 9.2.** *Crimestoppers: numbers of informers introduced into the Metropolitan Police informer system 1995–1999*

| Year | Number introduced |
|------|-------------------|
| 1995 | 32 |
| 1996 | 62 |
| 1997 | 58 |
| 1998 | 77 |
| 1999 | 72 |

*Source*: Metropolitan Police Crimestoppers Unit.

## What results are achieved?

Preserving the anonymity of Crimestoppers has proved to be exceptionally effective. Since its inception in the UK, Crimestoppers has achieved a steady increase in arrests year on year as outlined in Table 9.3 below, and a total of 34,082 arrests had been achieved by the end of 1999. These are results, it is suggested, that would not have been secured without Crimestoppers.

In 1999 alone Crimestoppers calls resulted in the arrest and charge of 38 people for murder, 22 for attempted murder, 13 for rape, 28 for firearms offences, 202 for robbery and 338 for burglary. More than 2,300 drug dealers were disrupted by arrest, many of them by Her Majesty's Customs and Excise officers, who also receive intelligence via Crimestoppers units.

**Table 9.3** *Arrests from Crimestoppers 1990–1999*

| Year | 1990 | 1991 | 1992 | 1993 | 1994 | 1995 | 1996 | 1997 | 1998 | 1999 |
|------|------|------|------|------|------|------|------|------|------|------|
| Arrests | 2,566 | 1,609 | 1,764 | 2,303 | 2,943 | 3,355 | 4,347 | 4,726 | 5,169 | 5,300 |

*Source*: Crimestoppers Trust

Research undertaken by the Metropolitan Police Service (MPS) provides further support for the effectiveness of the Crimestoppers operation (Monaghan, 1999). It shows that information coming into Crimestoppers is not, as is sometimes suggested, duplicating information retrievable from elsewhere in the intelligence system. Ninety-nine cases were sampled; all related to drug dealing activities. These 99 cases resulted in 139 arrests, and in 83 per cent of the cases there had been no prior intelligence. Only two of those arrested were classed as a 'prominent nominal' offenders within the MPS system. Of the 139 arrested, 107 (77 per cent) were males, and 32 (or 23 per cent) were females. Of the total, 78 (56 per cent) were known to have previous convictions; for 9 (7 per cent) there was no data on previous convictions. Of these 139 arrested suspects, 98 (71 per cent) were charged; the remainder were either cautioned or no action

**Table 9.4** *Results of Crimestoppers survey*

| | |
|---|---|
| Number of calls sampled | 99 |
| Resulting Arrests | 139 |
| Male suspects | 107 (77%) |
| Female suspects | 32 (23%) |
| Previous convictions | 78 (56%) |
| No previous convictions | 52 (37%) |
| Unknown | 9 (7%) |
| *Disposal* | |
| Charged | 98 (71%) |
| Cautioned | 35 (25%) |
| Formal warnings | 2 (1%) |
| No further action | 4 (3%) |
| *Recoveries* | |
| Class A drugs | 25% |
| Class B drugs | 75% |
| Section 1 firearms | 16 |
| Crimestoppers rewards paid | 10 |
| *Total reward payments* | £1,575 |

**Table 9.5**  *Value of Crimestoppers' information*

| Value of information | Number of answers | Percentage of answers |
|---|---|---|
| Crime was reported but the information was crucial to detection | 309 | (63%) |
| Information was useful but not critical | 133 | (27%) |
| Information was of little or no value | 25 | (5%) |
| Information was of little or no value due to anonymity | 5 | (1%) |
| Other aspects – police informant recruited | 19 | (4%) |
| *Total* | 491 | (100%) |

*Source:* Vauxhall Centre for the Study of Crime, the University of Luton

was taken. A considerable number of these offenders were involved in drug offences, the drugs recovered being mainly Class B although 33 (29 per cent) were Class A, mainly cocaine. The police also seized a number of firearms. Of these 99 cases, in 10 rewards were paid by Crimestoppers, the total amount paid out £1,575. This data is presented in tabular form above in Table 9.4.

**Table 9.6**  *Offenders revealed by Crimestoppers*

| Category of offender | Number of offenders | Percentage of offenders |
|---|---|---|
| Not previously known | 76 | (22%) |
| Known but not suspected of this offence | 141 | (41%) |
| Known and suspected of this offence | 128 | (37%) |
| *Total* | 345 | (100%) |

*Source*: Vauxhall Centre for the Study of Crime, the University of Luton

A more wide-ranging study has been conducted by the Vauxhall Centre for the Study of Crime at the University of Luton on behalf of the Crimestoppers Trust. The aim of this research was to determine the value of Crimestoppers to the public and police. This was done by measuring indicators of 'added value' which Crimestoppers information, obtained from anonymous informants made to police enquiries. Questionnaires were sent out through ten of the 29 Crimestoppers offices to police case officers who had received Crimestoppers information, and where the offender had been arrested and charged. A total of 345 officers returned the questionnaires; some gave more than one answer. Accordingly, Table 9.5

above lists the numbers of answers rather than officers, in other words 345 officers returned 491 assessments of value. Table 9.7 gives information on the manner in which the 345 police officers rate Crimestoppers information. Here it can be seen that 245 (or 74 per cent) rated it as very valuable (i.e. numbers 1 and 2 on the rating scale) whereas only 9 (or 2.3 per cent) rated it as of little value, i.e. numbers 6 and 7.

**Table 9.7**   *Police officers' views of Crimestoppers information*

| Value (scale 1–7) | | Number | Percentage |
|---|---|---|---|
| Very valuable | 1 | 133 | (39%) |
| | 2 | 121 | (35%) |
| | 3 | 45 | (13%) |
| | 4 | 24 | (7%) |
| | 5 | 14 | (4%) |
| | 6 | 7 | (2%) |
| Little value | 7 | 1 | (0.3%) |
| *Total* | | 345 | (100%) |

*Source*: Vauxhall Centre for the Study of Crime, the University of Luton

**Table 9.8**   *Crimestoppers: variance with previous two weeks before campaign*

| Type of calls | 1999 | 2000 |
|---|---|---|
| Actionable calls to Crimestoppers | +172% | +284% |
| Drug-related calls | +213% | +557% |

## 'Rat on a Rat' – a case study

Drugs misuse and crime are strongly connected. There are between 100,000 and 200,000 problem drug users in England and Wales, of whom about 50,000 to 60,000 are arrested and prosecuted within any given year. This group alone may each commit some 150 crimes a year – equivalent to 7.5 million offences – although a high proportion of this will go unrecorded by the police (Home Office, *ibid*). Around 30 per cent of arrestees say that they are currently dependent on one or more drugs (Home Office, *ibid*). It has been estimated that the proceeds of almost a third of acquisitive crime is geared to the purchase of heroin or crack cocaine.

Breaking the link between drug misuse and offending is another integral part of the Government's crime strategy. During 1999, 44 per cent of Crimestoppers generated arrests nationally were for drug-related offences (Crimestoppers Trust, 1999). In the London Metropolitan area alone 59 per cent of Crimestoppers generated arrests concerned drug related offences (Monaghan, 1999).

Operation Crackdown is the name given to the Metropolitan Police's offensive against drug misuse in the capital. Launched in May 1996, the campaign's aim is to arrest and prosecute dealers and to divert drug misusers towards appropriate treatment. Operation Crackdown is supported by the largest-ever advertising campaign to disrupt drug-dealing and the criminal activity associated with drugs. Crimestoppers is fundamental to this campaign, in that the advertising compares drug dealers to rats and urges the public to 'Rat on a Rat' by calling the freephone Crimestoppers number anonymously with information about drug dealers.

The most recent pan-London campaign, which ran during a two week period between 17 and 31 January 2000, had a substantial impact upon actionable calls being received by the MPS Crimestoppers unit. A summary of the results is shown in table 9.8 (MPS Crimestoppers Unit, 2000)

## Conclusion

Crimestoppers provides a significant benefit to UK law enforcement. It produces results that would not otherwise be secured and does so through a unique partnership with the community. Crimestoppers has flourished by public demand and support. The police service has a duty to ensure the future and growth of this positive contribution to crime reduction.

## References

Crimestoppers Trust (1999), unpublicised research carried out by Vauxhall Centre for the Study of Crime, University of Luton.

Home Office (1999) *The Government's Crime Strategy*, London: HMSO.

Metropolitan Police Service (1998) 'The London Beat', Directorate of Public Affairs.

Monaghan, G. (1999) 'Findings of Crimestoppers Analysis', Metropolitan Police Service, Crimestoppers Unit, unpublished report (MPS SO11 Branch, Directorate of Intelligence).

*The Criminal Procedure and Investigations Act* (1996), London: HMSO.

# 10 Informers and witness protection schemes

## Philip Bean

Not all informers require protection, and not all witnesses on protection schemes are informers. The common feature is that witnesses and informers (the latter are simply witnesses of a different sort), require protection of a nature and degree that is of a higher order. Witness intimidation has been defined as involving,

> threats to harm someone, acts to harm them, physical and financial harm, and acts against a third party (such as the relative of the witness) with the purpose of deterring the witness from reporting the crime in the first instance or deterring them from giving evidence in Court.
>
> (Home Office, 1998)

Witness intimidation has been classified in a number of different ways, some more complicated than others. One is called 'case specific intimidation'; that is it involves threats of violence, aimed at discouraging a person from helping with a particular investigation. Another is the so-called 'community intimidation' which covers acts intended to create an atmosphere of fear and non co-operation within a particular area of the community. A different classification is in social and cultural terms, where 'social intimidation' involves straightforward threats or acts of violence towards a witness, and 'cultural intimidation' occurs when friends and family of the witness try to dissuade the witness from assisting an investigation. Then there is 'perceived intimidation' which occurs when fear of intimidation is thought likely to occur but may not have occurred as yet (Home Office, 1998).

Warwick Maynard provides a less complicated classification, based simply on the levels of intimidation (Maynard, 1994). At the top is Tier 1, which is reserved for a small core of witnesses who need the strictest levels of police protection, and could involve 24-hour surveillance and may lead to relocation and a change of identity. Tier 2, the middle tier, is for those where the level of protection required is less, but where witnesses may suffer intimidation or harassment of a sufficient degree to suggest they are in some danger. At the bottom, Tier 3 is for those witnesses who have been discouraged from reporting offences to the police because of threats made to them and who feel intimidated.

The type of witness protection scheme that concerns us here is for witnesses in Tier 1, i.e. those needing the highest level of protection, and who may or may not be informers. All will be compromised, that is their identity will be known to the offenders, and the crimes about which they are witnesses will be serious: invariably serious crimes lead to serious intimidation. Informers do not retain their status when they become protected witnesses, for once admitted all links with their original handler are cut. All protected witnesses, whether informers or not, are given a new handler who works for the witness protection unit.

Only a small number of police forces in Britain have witness protection schemes – Greater Manchester, the Metropolitan Police and the Royal Ulster Constabulary being the most prominent. In London the protection of witnesses and informers has been under the control of the Metropolitan Police since the early 1970s. It is now under the control of the Organised Crime Group in the Criminal Justice Protection Unit (or CJPU).* It has responsibilities over and above protecting witnesses, including protecting juries, previously dealt with by other specialist operations and technical operations departments. Other police forces, including other agencies, may ask CJPU for assistance; that help may involve relocating witnesses, changing their identity and so on.

It is strange that a number of police forces in Britain have no trained officers to deal with witness protection, nor do they have their own schemes. Those without are not always the smallest forces; presumably they believe they do not have witnesses needing that level of protection, or if they do are prepared to buy into other more substantial schemes such as from the Metropolitan Police or elsewhere.

There has been some research on the way Tier 3 operates (Maynard, 1994), but none on Tiers 1 and 2. Research on Tier 3 was commissioned because of concern 'that the development of a constructive partnership between the police and the public was being hampered by the intimidation of witnesses.' (*ibid*). The purpose of that study was to estimate how widespread was the intimidation and to advise how it might be reduced. The results show that intimidation was highest in high crime housing estates where 13 per cent of crimes reported by victims, and 9 per cent reported by witnesses lead to subsequent intimidation. For those crimes not reported, 6 per cent are not reported by victims, and 22 per cent

---

* I am grateful for the help and assistance provided by those in the witness protection unit at New Scotland Yard and to others who for security reasons cannot be formally acknowledged yet who gave up their time to answer the many questions which a study of this nature generates. Most of the data for this chapter came from the Metropolitan Police Unit and may be less applicable to other units elsewhere.

are not reported by witnesses due to intimidation. When the offender knows the identity of the victim intimidation is difficult to prevent (*ibid*).

## Protected status

Protected status is the general title given to persons within the defined categories who have been accepted into the witness protection scheme. There are three forms of protected status. First, protected witnesses who can provide essential information about the most serious offences, and, whose safety is under substantial threat. Protected witnesses are not informers, that is they are not registered informers though they may well have been and have acted as registered informers in the past. Second, the protected informer who will be a registered informer who informs usually on his associates, whose identity is known to them and of whose safety there is also a substantial threat. Protected informers may have been participating informers, i.e. involved in criminal activity which was approved by the handler acting with additional approval from senior officers, and are unlikely to be charged with the crimes about which they have provided information. Third, there is the resident informer who after arrest or conviction, and usually before sentence, gives information about other criminals, and as a result is also under substantial threat. The resident informer will expect to receive a reduced sentence as a result of that information. To complicate matters further, the resident informer may have been a protected informer at an earlier stage in their career.

Protected witnesses, protected informers and resident informers, indeed all who enter witness protection schemes, do so on the undertaking that they will not act as informers. That would reduce the level of protection that could be provided – informers tend to return to the areas in which the crimes were committed. Once their identity has been compromised they are vulnerable. They will be given two official warnings after which they will be removed from the witness protection scheme should they not abide by the conditions of the scheme.

In the early 1970s, with the growth of armed robbery and other types of serious crimes, a new type of resident informer appeared – the Supergrass as they were called by the police (see Chapter 9 of this volume). The first was 'Bertie' Smalls who in return for immunity gave evidence against 32 armed robbers, all co-conspirators and fellow criminals. Others followed, many of them terrorists. Smalls was given total immunity; others were not, although this did not stop them coming forward, presumably in the hope of a reduction in the sentence. This type of offender dominated the earlier witness protection schemes. More recently they have given way to a new group, more likely to be involved in drug trafficking, and serious crimes such as homicides which result from drugs. There are also the international criminals who do not commit their offences in the countries in which they live, and even more recently the so-called 'bent' policeman who also seek a lighter sentence in exchange for information on colleagues. The sheer numbers of these offenders coming forward with their differing demands and expectations puts an additional strain on those providing the protection.

## Acquiring protected status

A witness protection scheme like that run by the Metropolitan Police would expect to receive about 400–500 applications per year. Only about half of these will be accepted; there is a tendency for witnesses to overstate the danger, and for police officers to overstate the importance of their witness. Of those 200 or so who are admitted family members must also be included; the average family is about 2.5 members, so about 500 people will enter the programme annually in London alone.

The standard admission procedure is detailed and lengthy. The first stage is to determine whether the applicants fit the criteria. If so, then applicants are given a risk assessment to determine the nature and level of risk, and as part of that assessment to determine whether financial or technical help is required. Where the applicants are not successful assistance is given about how best to cope with their level of intimidation. Once accepted into the scheme witnesses remain until it is safe to leave, as of course do their family members. On arrival all witnesses are debriefed; this can be a lengthy process taking two years or more. Resident informers, i.e. those in prison, may be debriefed either in the prison system, or may be kept in special units in police stations under a so-called Production Order (this is under Section 29 of the Criminal Justice Act 1991 or under Rule 6 of the Prison Rules 1964). After debriefing those not in prison will be sent to safe houses (the CJPU prefer the term 'temporary accommodation', that is a house not attributed to the police). These may be owned by the witnesses, or rented from the local council, or from a local housing association. In very serious cases the witness will be sent abroad.

A number of measures need to be taken, and obstacles overcome, if those in the witness protection scheme are to have their identity preserved. Some are straightforward and practical, but no less important for that. For example, in the early stages, perhaps before being admitted to the scheme, it would be unwise for the police to visit the witnesses' home immediately after the crime, and should a visit be needed it would be best if made by a plain clothes officer. Another approach is to make house-to-house calls on all surrounding properties to help avoid drawing attention to a particular witness. Encounters between witnesses and offenders in the police station are to be avoided at all costs. All this may seem obvious but small mistakes can have disastrous consequences, and ruin what is otherwise a carefully planned operation. Intimidation does not end at the point where the offender is convicted and imprisoned, for there remains a risk of retaliation from friends and family. Offenders in prison may still direct intimidation from inside, or they may wait until they are released. Those who are members of organised crime syndicates always remain a threat; they have long memories it seems.

## Resident informers

A resident informer is a witness with protected status who has been arrested, possibly also convicted, and is detained within the criminal justice system, whether in prison or on probation or on parole. The Home Office gives a more expansive definition:

> A resident informer is an active participant in a serious crime or a succession of serious crimes who after arrest or conviction elects to identify, give evidence against and provide intelligence about fellow criminals involved in those or other offences.
>
> (Home Office, 1992)

For the purposes of this definition 'serious crime' means crime which can attract a long prison sentence. 'Resident informer' is not a precise term – it can be applied to non-residents, i.e. on probation, or on parole – but it permits a distinction to be made between these and participating informers who may be active and are not arrested or convicted. Resident informers can expect the same range of sentences as other offenders but in practice about 90 per cent are sent to prison.

Resident informers must wait for the sentences to be passed on those on whom they have informed before receiving their own. The court will want to see the quality of their information before deciding, and it will not want the informer to receive protected status and then change his mind. The resident informer, having admitted his part in the crimes and expecting a reduced sentence, may find himself in the paradoxical position of being the only one sent to prison should the others be found not guilty.

Those receiving a prison sentence will serve it in one of the special units within the prison system (the position of women resident informers is more complicated as the numbers are small and no units are available. See the Chapter 6 by Teresa Nemitz). These units are too small to provide the range of services other prisoners receive, and living with a small number of similarly placed prisoners cannot be other than a limiting experience. It is not uncommon for resident informers to receive long sentences, of ten years or more. Category A prisoners, i.e. those who themselves present danger were they to escape, cannot go on witness protection schemes as there is a lack of suitable security in the units for them.

Resident informers in the community, i.e. those on probation or on parole, generate unique problems for the probation services, especially when required to prepare pre-sentence reports or to undertake the supervision. For obvious reasons, resident informers will not discuss their offence, their family background, their current family situation or any matter that could link them to an earlier life. Their names may have been changed so they will not appear on any police or court records. The standard information required for a pre-sentence report or a parole assessment therefore will not be available, and should they be placed on probation or granted parole the local police will not know their current status. Some may be granted a special dispensation allowing them not to report to the probation office, others may be sent abroad and avoid supervisory contacts altogether. Protecting their identity is paramount; the system operates on the basis that the fewer people that know the better. Hence the proposal from CJPU to move towards a dedicated unit with specialist probation officers who will prepare the reports, undertake the supervision, and of equal importance, provide an input into the prison units in the form of training programmes, therapies, and so on. At present CJPU officers sometimes undertakes the supervision, at the behest of the local probation service, with the CJPU handler reporting direct to the local probation officer.

## Special categories and facilities

Relocating witnesses abroad requires producing new passports, visas, National Insurance numbers (or the equivalent) and an agreement from the host country to receive the witness and his family. In turn Britain provides reciprocal arrangements for other countries to receive their protected witnesses here. There is no available data on the numbers sent abroad or received in Britain.

The increasingly international nature of crime adds to the complexity of what is already a complex enterprise. Foreign nationals who would normally not qualify for entry into Britain due to their criminal connections, whether here or elsewhere, may have useful information about criminal activities within Britain, and be prepared to act as an informer. Or there may be someone subject to a deportation order, or who is refused admission perhaps as an illegal immigrant, or who does not qualify for asylum, yet who also shows a willingness to act as an informer. These will be of interest to the law enforcement agencies, not just the police but Customs and Excise too. The immigration services must be involved for they must make the final decision whenever a foreign national is to be given entry. Liaising with the immigration services is the responsibility of the police who must provide full details of the witness. Some spectacular successes have occurred but so too have there been spectacular failures, one of which involved a Jamaican national who had numerous previous convictions, including violence. He was allowed into Britain to inform against the 'Yardies'. Unfortunately he was handled by a junior officer in the Metropolitan Police and came to Nottingham where he was caught committing other offences including supplying drugs and serious violence. It is not just a matter of protecting witnesses but of protecting others who may be the witnesses' victims.

## Successes and failures

Assessing success and failure is difficult: in rather crude terms success means the witness remains protected for as long as is necessary, and failure means otherwise. Success and failure must also be defined in terms of the witnesses' family. Success also means that the witness gives truthful evidence leading to the conviction of one or more offenders, does not return to crime whilst on the witness protection programme, and does not engage in behaviour which leads to the new identity being compromised, such as returning to old criminal haunts. Failure means the opposite: it means failing to give evidence, truthful or not, which does not lead to the conviction of one or more offenders; being involved in crime whilst on the witness protection scheme; and behaving in ways which compromise the existing identity. (There are many cautionary tales as to what happens to witnesses taken off the scheme, especially if involved with organised crime syndicates. The speed with which their fate is sealed adds to the caution). Some witnesses, it has to be accepted, are unprotectable, whether through no fault of their own, or because of the circumstances in which they find themselves, or simply because they cannot keep away from crime. In a curious twist of fate, information about failures almost always comes to the witness protection unit by way of other informers.

The CJPU claim they run a successful witness protection programme but publish no figures about success or failure. Their message is simple; those witnesses who abide by the rules will remain protected, those who do not must expect the consequences. The US Witness Security Program also claims success, saying:

> On balance the Witness Security Program is a very successful operation. Information provided by protected witnesses helped to convict more than 89 per cent of the defendants against whom they have testified.... Not only do witnesses feel safe to speak out against their confederates but in the majority of cases they go and live normal lives. This is no small accomplishment, in that more than 97 per cent have extensive criminal records. Some do return to crime but only between 17 per cent and 23 per cent. This rate of recidivism among program participants is less than half the rate of those released from the nations prisons.
>
> (US Department of Justice, 1988: 7)

That many protected witnesses, particularly informers, have previous convictions adds to the problems. Failure rates are always higher for offender populations, and those offenders with the most convictions invariably have the highest rate of failure – that is so whether they are informers or not. Witness protection schemes will, on this point alone, have high-risk populations with an expectation that many would have continued to commit crime. Determining success must take this into account.

The witnesses must adjust to a life free of crime, perhaps abroad, but certainly in a new district of Britain, and that also means getting a job, perhaps for the first time (the US Department of Justice notes that it is extremely important that the witness finds something to occupy their time, preferably obtaining employment as soon as possible, adding that a job builds confidence and helps the witness feel they are once again in control and supporting their family (*ibid*)). It almost always means a measure of downward mobility, informers are likely to have made more money as informers than they would in legitimate occupations. In witness protection they may live in rented accommodation instead of the superior detached residence they may have been used to, they may at best have a second-hand car instead of a new one, the children may go to local schools instead of the private schools, and so on. For the informer this may not seem like success. Measuring success, however, is not about making comparisons with a previous lifestyle but about adjusting to the new one, which, if only to repeat the point, will, according to the CJPU, be successful if the witnesses follow the CJPU guidelines.

Few resident informers are easy to protect on release from prison but those that turn out to be the most difficult to protect are the ex-policemen. Many were convicted whilst acting as serving police officers and may also have informed on colleagues in return for a lighter sentence. They themselves might have been the victims of informers – the link between corrupt police officers and informers is set out clearly in Chapter 2 in this volume. They may retain links with the offender population outside the prison, and may also retain links with some colleagues in the police; they know and have operated on both sides. This will make them a formidable group to handle. Their manner and demeanour make it difficult to hide their identity, making it additionally hard for them to merge into a new social world. Seeking out old colleagues, whether offenders or police officers, could be especially dangerous.

## Some concluding comments

No details are available, nationally or otherwise, of the costs of the various programmes, nor can comparisons be made between the programmes provided by the different police forces. The per capita base is thought to be high; resettlement and relocation can never be cheap, and if the witness goes abroad resettlement will cost more. Some witnesses may remain protected for life, others for shorter periods. The greatest costs are likely to be in the early stages, where financial and other assistance may be required until an adjustment is made to a new way of life. Having encouraged these witnesses to give evidence the financial cost is the price the State pays to keep its side of the bargain.

Measuring cost-effectiveness is always going to be difficult where the key variables, which could defray the costs, remain uncertain. For example assume there is a high profile murder enquiry which has already run for over 12 months, and at a cost thus far of £6–£7million. An informer would have shortened the enquiry and reduced the cost dramatically, making the informer system and the ensuing protected witness scheme extremely cost-effective. Not all cases are as dramatic, but the point can be made that informers may help reduce the costs of policing, and witness protection is the price to be paid for that system. Nor is it ever easy to determine the price of justice; if an informer helps convict a serious offender it is difficult to see how to determine whether the cost of that is appropriate to the offender's sentence.

It is likely that every major crime in Britain, whether it be a drug case, a bank robbery, or a high-level fraud, and every major success against organised crime will depend on an informer. It is likely too that witness protection will be required for a number of these witnesses. How many and for how long is not known, nor is it known in advance how long those under witness protection will be required to remain in the programme. This is not to avoid questions about cost; some practices may be more cost-effective than others, we simply do not know.

Understandably, the police have hitherto been reluctant to talk about witness protection schemes and indeed about informers generally. That a new openness has arisen is to be welcomed; the police need to be reassured that researchers will not compromise their programmes nor compromise those witnesses and others working within it. Yet no organisation should remain so secretive as to be outside the boundaries of critical evaluation. Questions need to be asked and answers given in such a way as to retain the integrity of the organisation yet not leave it shrouded in mystery. The more secretive the organisation the more suspicious outsiders will be of it, leading to an even greater level of suspicion within the organisation. Suspicion can easily lead to accusations that things are not as they should be, and a downward spiral begins. Witness protection is too important for that to happen.

The type of questions to be asked falls into a number of different categories. Firstly, there are those of cost: what does the witness protection programme cost, is it adequately funded, is it for lack of funding turning people away who it would not otherwise, and would an increase in funding produce more witnesses; and if so, what would be the financial cost of such an extension? Secondly, is the programme adequately staffed, is it drawing too narrow a line as to who should be admitted, is the supervision system adequate (statutory or otherwise), is the detention system appropriate, is the risk assessment adequate, and is there satisfactory co-operation from other agencies? Thirdly, there are questions relating to people currently outside the scheme at Tier 2 and 3. Are we doing enough for those whose level of intimidation is not sufficient to bring them into the programme, but whose fear is real even if others may not see things that way? There are many people living in high crime areas who find levels of abuse, verbal and otherwise, intimidating yet may not be given the appropriate help. What can be done for these people, and how best can we improve their position? These questions are by no means all that need to be asked, but addressing them might help the current programme. And again, if only to repeat the point that some police forces in Britain have neither a witness protection scheme nor a trained officer – perhaps the first question to be asked is why this is so.

Whatever one may think of the murky world in which informants move, without them many serious offenders would not be convicted and much serious crime would remain undetected. If informers are to be encouraged to come forward there must be a protection scheme to protect them when things go wrong. That scheme must operate according to the highest standards of secrecy, for where there are weaknesses there will be serious consequences for all concerned. One such consequence will be a reduction in the levels of confidence generated for would-be informers, and a lack of trust means they will not come forward.

Some commentators see a compelling need for legislation by making it an offence 'to trace, cause to be traced, or to reveal without leave of a Crown Court judge any individual whose identity has been protected by statutory provision'. This, it is said, would underscore the value placed on witnesses and informers. Whether it would achieve what was hoped for is another matter. Clearly, the demand for protection will not go away nor is there likely to be a reduction in intimidation, at least in the near future. Currently witness protection is dealt with in the Police and Criminal Evidence Act 1984 (PACE). That may not be sufficient.

# References

Home Office (1992) *Resident Informers* (Circular 9/1992).

Home Office (1998) *Speaking up for Justice* (June).

Maynard, W. (1994) *Witness Intimidation: strategies for prevention.* Crime Detection and Prevention Series, Paper 55, Police Research Group.

US Department of Justice (United States Marshalls Service) (1988) 'Testifying without Reprisal', *The Pentacle*, Winter, Vol. 8, no. 8: 3–7.

# 11 Regulating informers:

## the Regulation of Investigatory Powers Act, covert policing and human rights

## Peter Neyroud and Alan Beckley

Since modern policing in the UK began, there has been no formal legal framework for the regulation of informers. Whilst 'informers' have been a staple of the world of police fiction, in the world of police 'fact' the criminal justice system has usually tacitly and only, fitfully, acknowledged their existence (Rose, 1996). However, the increasing importance of covert policing through the 1990s, the strong encouragement for the use of 'informants' in official reports (Audit Commission, 1993), the consequent movement towards 'intelligence-led' policing and a widespread concern about miscarriages of justice had begun to raise questions as to why such covert methods were not properly regulated.

The first approach to such regulation came from the courts, supported by primary legislation such as Section 78 of the Police and Criminal Evidence Act 1984 (PACE). This sought to deal with the concerns about 'agents provocateurs' and 'deals with criminals' by becoming more active in developing rules of exclusion for evidence that appeared to be tainted by informer involvement (Robertson, 1989). This has been an essentially permissive regime which has accorded well with Skolnick's thesis that deception in criminal investigation could be considered acceptable up to the doors of the interview room and no further and, above all, not in the trial process (Skolnick, 1975). This regime has provided very few formal rules for the investigating team in the intelligence-gathering and investigative phase. It has concentrated on ensuring the fairness of the trial by demanding greater disclosure, in particular the need to disclose monetary rewards.

The implementation of the Human Rights Act 1998 (HRA) and thereby Article 2 to 12 and 14 of the European Convention on Human Rights (ECHR) has required a radical rethink of this first approach and provided a compelling need for a formal legislative framework governing all three phases. Instead of looking at police actions from the viewpoint of the criminal justice process only, the Human Rights Act demands that law enforcement actions are examined from the viewpoint of the citizen. Hence, interference with the latter's rights to 'private and family life'

(Article 8, ECHR) through a deceptive relationship with an informer will now require a 'clear legal basis' whether or not the interference results in a subsequent court case. In order to secure the continued development of an area of policing that this book has shown to be vital, the UK government were left with little choice but to find a formal legal instrument to underpin the police use of informers. The Regulation of Investigatory Powers Act 2000 (RIPA) was, therefore, drafted and hastened through Parliament just in time to beat the October 2000 deadline for the HRA.

This chapter will discuss RIPA, describing its main provisions and the way in which its framework has been constructed. In particular, we will concentrate on Part II of the Act and the new concept of 'Covert Human Intelligence Sources' (CHIS). We will analyse the Act as a means of securing 'compliance' with human rights law, drawing specifically on the work that the human rights organisation Justice completed on surveillance policing and human rights (Justice, 1998) and on our own work on 'ethical policing' (Neyroud and Beckley, 2000). We will then seek to gauge the likely impact of the Act on the way in which police use informers by examining the lessons of the last major legislative change in UK policing – the introduction of the PACE Act in 1985.

## The Regulation of Investigatory Powers Act and 'Covert Human Intelligence Sources'

The Regulation of Investigatory Powers Act (RIPA) is the culmination of a great deal of work by the Association of Chief Police Officers and non-governmental organisations (NGOs) such as Justice (1998) to improve the controls and culture of 'covert policing'. The Act seeks to provide a clear statutory regime for areas of policing that have previously been regulated only by Home Office circulars and internal guidance, and updates legislation such as the Interception of Communication Act 1985 which has been criticised by the European Court. The Act breaks down into four main parts:

- Communication data (Part 1)

- Surveillance (Part II)

- Electronic data and encryption (Part III)

- The scrutiny process (Part IV)

Part II divides surveillance further into three parts: Directed; Intrusive; and Covert Human Intelligence Sources. Whilst it is the latter and its accompanying Code of Practice which directly concern us here, it is important to stress that the Codes and the authorisation processes acknowledge the very clear operational links between different types of covert policing.

Instead of seeking to define 'informers' by their evidential or intelligence outcome, RIPA turns the concept on its head and uses the 'covert relationship' with the subject as the key. As such there is a substantial shift from ethics of utility and a concentration on results to the ethics of duty and a greater concern with the propriety of the process and the human dignity of the subject (Neyroud and Beckley, 2000). In the case of informers, their subject is accorded, in their private and family life, a 'reasonable expectation of privacy'. Hence, when through a deceptive relationship, an informer 'covertly uses the relationship to obtain information...or covertly discloses information obtained by the use of such a relationship...' (Section 26(8)), this can be 'construed as an infringement' of the suspect's rights (Code of Practice, paragraph 1.4).[1]

Having established the point of infringement, RIPA pursues the logic of human rights principles.

- Legality: the necessity for a clear and accessible legal basis for the public authority to interfere with rights. In this case the accessibility of the new guidelines are considerably enhanced by the creation of publicly accessible Codes of Practice setting out the boundaries of police action, the authorisation process and the accountability system.

- Proportionality: 'before authorising the use or conduct of a source, the authorising officer should first satisfy himself that the likely degree of intrusion into the privacy of those potentially affected is proportionate to what the use or conduct of the source seeks to achieve' (Section 29(b) and Code of Practice, paragraph 2.5).

- Necessity: covert sources can only be authorised for the purposes defined in Article 8, such as 'the prevention or detection of crime or for the prevention of disorder'.

- Remedy: a new process of independent oversight by the Surveillance Commissioners together with a Tribunal to hear complaints and actions for redress. This provides the citizen with their main avenue for the 'redress' required by Section 7 of the HRA where a breach of ECHR can be demonstrated.

Around these principles the legislators have then laid the detail of the administrative and oversight processes that law enforcement agencies[2] must follow. Firstly, the key building block is that the 'Use and conduct' of a CHIS must be the subject of prior authorisation by a senior officer[3] who is, as far as possible, separate from the controlling or handling of the source (Code of Practice, paragraph 2.10). The definition of 'Covert Human Intelligence Source' includes both informers and covert police officers, because the infringement of rights – a deceptive relationship – is similar in kind (paragraph 2.16).

There have always been, as this book suggests, particular problems with 'participant' and 'juvenile' informants. RIPA caters indirectly for the former – those who may be involved in crime as a result of their tasking – by permitting tasking which 'may involve the source in infiltrating an existing criminal conspiracy' (paragraph 2.11). The extent of this involvement, which was previously circumscribed by case law and Home Office Circulars, is not developed in the Act or Code of Practice. 'Juvenile sources' are covered by tighter rules that specifically exclude those 'under 16 years of age and living with his parents being authorised to give information against his or her parents' (paragraph 2.25) and a higher authority level (paragraph 2.27).

There are carefully prescribed management disciplines. Authorisations are provided for up to 12 months without renewal. This is considerably longer than the 3 months' limit for intrusive surveillance authorities and recognises the often prolonged nature of the informer relationship (paragraph 2.35). Management of sources must include a designated handler, who is responsible for day-to-day running, and a designated controller, who must ensure that the risk assessment process is up to date and that proper records are being kept (paragraphs 3.5-3.11). The whole process is now subjected to external oversight by Commissioners, who are granted powers to inspect any authorisation and to request any documents or information in connection with that inspection (paragraphs 3.16–4.2).

These arrangements, apart from the overlaying of the Commissioners, are very similar to those set out in the Codes that ACPO developed together with the Customs and Excise (ACPO, 1999). They are rather more restrictive in respect of juvenile informants and fight shy of detailed consideration of the question of informers or undercover officers participating in crime in the course of their relationship with the subject. The latter caused considerable debate amongst practitioners in the drafting of the Bill and the Codes, not least because the issue of participation has long been one of the most contentious, alongside the connected matter of 'deals' with informers. The absence of clear ethical guidelines in these areas within RIPA provides yet another argument for the rapid development of such guidelines by the police service (Neyroud and Beckley, 2000).

## RIPA and compliance

One of the key aims of the RIPA was to secure human rights compliance for areas of covert policing that had previously relied on the common law rule that 'whatever is not expressly forbidden by law is permissible' (Cheney *et al*, 1999:64). We will turn now to an analysis of the extent to which RIPA has achieved this.

In a seminal study of covert policing in the UK, Justice, the human rights NGO, analysed the existing common law framework against the principles of human rights (Justice, 1998).[4] Justice made four major recommendations on the police use of informers: juvenile informers should be the exception rather than the norm; there should be clearer rules on the granting of immunity to informers; there should be a primary legislative framework setting out the principles of police use of informers; and this framework should be supported by detailed Codes, which pay 'greater attention to the ethical issues in all areas'(p.109).

If we compare this to our description of the main provisions of RIPA, it is clear that the Act goes only part way to meet Justice's recommendations. Although there will now be a statutory framework and Code, there is less attention than Justice suggested to ethical guidance and stating the principles and rather greater concentration on managerial and administrative processes. Some of this missing detail may well be covered in the internal manuals which will support the Act and Code, but it would have had more weight had it been placed in the public domain and endorsed by Parliament.

In Justice's human rights analysis of the Bill for the second reading, they raised two other major issues (Justice, 2000). Firstly, 'Covert Human Intelligence Sources' ('CHIS') as an umbrella definition lumps a trained undercover police officer together with a criminal informer. This lack of distinction fails to distinguish the very different risks presented by the two, particularly when it comes to considering the issue of participation in crime. Furthermore, the Act and Code are, as we have seen above, fairly reticent in their guidance in this controversial area.

Justice's second issue related specifically to participation in crime. They argued that 'participating informers' and those whose tasking could be considered particularly intrusive need an authorisation process that is properly independent from the operational team and preferably judicial.

A second way of looking at RIPA and compliance is to examine the extent to which it contributes to what we have called elsewhere 'the compliance framework' (Neyroud and Beckley, 2000). This brings together the statutory, operational and managerial requirements that are necessary for a public authority to be able to demonstrate that its overall approach is 'compliant' with human rights and is, therefore, 'lawful'. There are two major elements to compliance: internal management and control systems; external accountability.

**Table 11.1** *A framework of compliance for police use of informers*

|  | Compliance requirement | Source of compliance |
|---|---|---|
| **Tactical operation**<br><br>*The day-to-day implementation and management of police use of informers* | • Manual of standards on covert policing<br>• Trained staff (such as informant handlers and controllers)<br>• Record-keeping and audit trails<br>• Leadership, supervision and support | • ACPO Manuals of guidance on management of informants (ACPO, 1999b)<br>• RIPA Codes of Practice |
| **Strategic**<br><br>*Chief Officer management and control of police use of informers* | • Intelligence/covert policing strategy<br>• Nationally agreed standards<br>• National training standards<br>• Control and audit systems<br>• Integrity control<br>• Leadership | • ACPO Manuals of guidance on management of informants (ACPO 1999b)<br>• RIPA Codes of Practice |
| **Legal and Societal**<br><br>*The legal and societal control systems* | • Clear and comprehensive legislative provision with supporting guidance<br>• Independent oversight/audit of applications and operations<br>• An independent Complaints system<br>• Public consultation about the nature and extent of covert policing<br>• Democratic oversight of covert policing | • RIPA 2000 and the accompanying Codes of Practice under both Acts<br>• The Commissioner system (RIPA) and HMIC inspections<br>• Tribunal system (RIPA) and Police Complaints system<br>• PCCGs set up under Section 106 Police and Criminal Evidence Act<br>• Parliamentary scrutiny of the Commissioner (RIPA) and the Police Authority |
| **Ethical principles**<br><br>*The ethical principles which must underpin covert policing* | • Respect for personal autonomy<br>• Beneficence and non-maleficence<br>• Justice<br>• Responsibility<br>• Care<br>• Honesty<br>• Stewardship | • Ethical Code for Police officers and guidance on ethics in covert policing (in preparation by ACPO) |

Table adapted from Neyroud and Beckley, 2000

Figure 11.1 draws these issues together and sets them out in the form of a 'model of compliance' with ethical and human rights principles. At first sight the model indicates that the UK has, with the implementation of RIPA, a strong framework. However, it is important to look behind the formal framework.

## Internal

There are four main areas of internal controls which are relevant to police use of informers: frontline supervision; internal guidelines and authorisation procedures; performance management; integrity testing. The first, frontline supervision, could be enhanced by RIPA, which offers, in the Codes, considerable opportunities for managerial intervention. Furthermore, the National Intelligence model requires greater involvement from senior uniform managers in the tasking process (NCIS, 2000). Their lack of involvement has been a crucial factor in many of the major scandals involving informers (Van Traa, 1996). Guidelines and authorisation procedures have been shown to be an important and effective element in limiting officers' discretion (Maguire and Norris, 1992). We will return below to the possible professionalising influence of the new RIPA framework.

Performance management of covert policing has proved especially difficult. RIPA, with its emphasis on detailed record keeping could be used to enhance the sort of quantitative management that risks encouraging borderline practices. A move away from a managerialist approach to a more professional, standards-based and qualitative methodology is particularly important in this area. Last, but not least, integrity testing of key staff is, as a number of chapters of this book stress, a vital part of any effective police management. RIPA provides a legal framework that ensures such testing can also be 'lawful' and compliant.

## External

There are several dimensions to the external framework: legislation, where we have seen already that RIPA provides a reasonable solution; democratic control; inspection and audit; Commissioner oversight; complaints procedures. Taking them in order, democratic control is limited by both the tripartite structure that restricts police authority intervention in 'operations', and the secrecy of those operations, with a consequent lack of information about their conduct and outputs. RIPA will significantly enhance the information that can be shared in Authorities and the information that will be scrutinised by Parliament, through the presentation of the Commissioners' reports. There is, moreover, scope for Forces to develop the way that they share information about the nature and control of covert operations through local consultation processes.

Inspection and audit have been important in promoting good practice (Audit Commission, 1993 and ACPO, 1996) and may well be enhanced by the mandated record-keeping and managerial systems that will be open to view. There is no requirement for prior approval by a Commissioner in the case of 'CHIS' authorisations in contrast to the regime that will govern other forms of intrusive covert policing. Complaints procedures are in the form of referral to a tribunal. The latter approach has been criticised for a lack of transparency and teeth in an analysis of the workings of the Security Service body (Justice, 2000). Justice have questioned how a citizen can seek an effective remedy when, in many cases, they will be unaware that their rights have been affected. One solution to this, which has been adopted in a number of countries, is a duty to disclose covert activity where it is subsequently clear that the suspect has not been involved. There is considerable reluctance from law enforcement agencies to pursue this course, because of the fears that such disclosures would harm future operations by sharing knowledge of operational tactics. Furthermore, the evidence that this would add significantly to the citizen's rights is, at best, limited.

If we take our two analyses together, we can see some clear common threads. The statutory framework brings a part of policing that was completely out of view into a sharper public focus. The new mandatory authorisation procedures should provide clear evidence of procedural compliance in a standard form that will allow inspection and oversight to be much improved both internally and externally. There are dangers that the rich information potential of the new system may be misused in the search for simple performance criteria about an area of policing where quality and professional judgement will always be more important than statistics.

RIPA has some shortfalls. The most obvious of these is the limited treatment of the crucial issue of 'participating informants'. A second one, which is less obvious and to which we have not yet alluded, is that RIPA takes a very British approach to legislating on informers. Twenty years ago this would not have presented any difficulties. Since then there has been a rapid growth of transnational policing, in response to transnational crime, particularly in the areas of drugs and organised crime. Policing these types of crimes inevitably involves the management of covert operations across European and international frontiers. It remains to be seen whether RIPA's approach, which differs so markedly from other continental models in key areas such as prior judicial oversight, will prove acceptable in those jurisdictions. This is a challenge to come and one which may well prove an important debate for those seeking to take the Tampere agreements on police and judicial cooperation forward (Justice, 2000b).

## RIPA and PACE: the implications of legislated change

In 1985 the PACE Act 1984 heralded one of the most significant changes in British policing by providing a new legislative framework to govern police powers of arrest, search and detention. The Act was controversial at the time, but has since become an international standard of good practice. In the Home Office Study 'PACE Ten Years On', Brown (1997) commented that 'it is implicit in PACE and the fine level of detailed rules and guidance in the accompanying Codes of Practice that those who drew up the legislation placed faith in the capacity of legal rules to influence police conduct' (p. 250). In contrast, Brown concluded, from his review of all the research on PACE, that there is no simple relationship between laws and police conduct. The extent to which the latter is impacted depends on a number of factors, in particular 'the relationship of the rules to existing working practices and the way that the rules are enforced'. The research also suggested that practices inside the police station, where there was more supervision and greater controls (such as CCTV), were more affected than practices outside the police station where there tended to be greater discretion. Furthermore, where the powers themselves were not clearly set out and where the training in exercising them was insufficient, such as stop and search powers, the impact was particularly diluted (Dixon *et al*, 1989). Last but not least, in many cases, procedures were followed without the substance or spirit of the legislation being properly complied with.

The key messages of Brown's review can be summarised succinctly as follows: legal rules can alter police practice as long as: they are clear; there is adequate training (and we might add that the training must be adequately followed up); there are effective sanctions; there is effective supervision; and the public are aware of their rights and police powers. To these issues we might add the need for rules to work within the organisational culture and to be reinforced by key leaders at all levels. As Chan (1997) has demonstrated, the external environment – including legislation – is only one component of effective change in policing.

If we compare these messages to the debate we have set out above on RIPA, we can suggest that PACE has a number of clear lessons for its successor and for the leaders of the service seeking to manage its introduction. Firstly, the lack of clarity in key areas of the legislation, which we have already highlighted in discussing 'participating informants', needs addressing in the internal guidance and careful monitoring. Secondly, there are already concerns about the speed with which the Act is being introduced, in contrast to PACE for which all forces launched a major training programme. Whilst the haste of action was a necessary product of the introduction of the Human Rights Act, the training will be a key determinant of whether the new Act embeds old practices or shifts law enforcement agencies to a new culture based on human rights. The latter requires a commitment to evidenced decision making and personal accountability which will prove uncomfortable for many practitioners without effective training and long-term development (Neyroud and Beckley, 2000).

Thirdly, RIPA demands a great deal of the handler and controller. Inevitably this will push police forces faster down the road to professionalisation of the intelligence function. This process, akin to the development of the custody officer's role post-PACE, is already being advanced by the National Intelligence model (NCIS, 2000). Dedicated Source Units, accredited handlers and controllers, better training for senior managers and a return to a more specialised detective branch after a number of years of toying with automatic tenure policies seems inevitable and desirable. The development of effective sanctions and the assurance of integrity will also drive every force to adopt a much more proactive stance to detecting, indeed anticipating, misconduct amongst those managing informers. The lessons of PACE are that such structural changes are essential to change the culture, which has too long been an 'entrepreneurial' one (Hobbs, 1988) rather than a professional one.

Finally, there has been little attempt to develop public understanding of this area of police work. Indeed, there have been conscious attempts, until very recently to keep the public at arms length from covert policing. In other areas of policing independent advisors are becoming one route to public participation and audit of controversial areas of policing. Whilst this is more difficult in the case of police use of informers, it is not impossible. The lessons of PACE are that public awareness and involvement, even at a relatively general level, can both challenge practice and conversely impact positively on public understanding of and, therefore, confidence in policing.

## Conclusions

RIPA is a very important piece of legislation. It provides the police and other public authorities with a legal framework that will enable them to use covert methods and an opportunity to do so in a way that meets human rights standards. As such RIPA is something of an experiment. There are few international examples of a legislated framework for the use of informers. On the whole most governments have chosen only to expose to public debate those aspects of covert policing that have resulted in scandal. RIPA has not sprung from such origins but rather from a desire amongst the senior police professionals to avoid such problems, which has coincided with pressure from civil liberties NGOs for change. This is an unusual partnership that has been further developed in the auditing of human rights compliance (Neyroud and Beckley, 2000). It offers a new partnership that might add significantly to the external influences on policing as it seeks to embed RIPA.

For the latter to succeed in developing new standards, there will need to be a combination of effective leadership within the service and constructive challenges from outside it. In particular, there will need to be a proper training strategy that encompasses Chief Officers, Senior Investigating Officers, Controllers, Handlers and Intelligence staff. Furthermore, the nature of RIPA and its origins in human rights mean that such training must rehearse the ethical debates that will be necessary for effective decision-making in this new era of covert policing.

## Notes

1 The references to the Code of Practice in this chapter are to the Code on 'the use of covert human intelligence sources' in the final consultation draft published by the Home Office on their website www.homeoffice.gov.uk/ripa.

2 The Code also applies to any 'public authority' (paragraph 1.1).

3 The precise levels of authorisation will range from an Inspector for urgent cases up to a Chief Constable where sensitive information may be involved.

4 One of the authors was a member of the Justice working party which advised on the drafts of the report.

## References

ACPO (1996) *Tackling Crime Effectively: Handbook Vol. II.* London: ACPO, HMIC, Home Office and Audit Commission.

ACPO (1999) *National Standards for Covert Policing.* London: ACPO.

Audit Commission (1993) *Helping with Enquiries.* Police Paper No. 12: London: HMSO.

Brown, D. (1997) *PACE Ten Years On: a review of the research*, Home Office Research Study No. 115, London: Home Office.

Chan, J.B.L. (1997) *Changing Police Culture: policing in a multi-cultural society.* Cambridge: CUP.

Cheney, D., Dickson, L., Fitzpatrick, J. and Uglow, S. (1999) *Criminal Justice and the Human Rights Act 1998.* Bristol: Jordans.

Hobbs, D. (1988) *Doing the Business: entrepreneurship, the working class and detectives in the East End of London.* Oxford: Oxford University Press.

Justice (1998) *Under Surveillance.* London: Justice.

Justice (2000) *The Regulation of Investigatory Powers Bill: briefing paper.* London: Justice.

Justice (2000b) *Annual Report.* London: Justice.

Maguire, M. and Norris, C. (1992) *The Conduct and Supervision of Criminal Investigations* London: HMSO, Royal Commission on Criminal Justice, Research Study No. 5.

NCIS (2000) *National Intelligence Model.* London: National Criminal Intelligence Service.

Neyroud, P.W. and Beckley, A. (2000) *Policing, Ethics and Human Rights.* Exeter: Willan.

Robertson, G. (1989) *Freedom, the Individual and the Law.* Harmondsworth: Penguin.

Rose, D. (1996) *In the Name of the Law: the collapse of criminal justice.* London: Jonathan Cape.

Skolnick, J. (1975) *Justice without Trial.* Second Edition, New York: Wiley.

Van Traa, M. (1996) *Report of the Parliamentary Enquiry Committee concerning Investigation methods.* Translation of article from *the Nederlands Juristenblad,* 9 February, No.6.

# Index